T5-CCT-946

Autobiography of a Georgia Cat

by

Michael Cowl Gordon

This book is a work of fiction. Places, events, and situations in this story are purely fictional. Any resemblance to actual persons, living or dead, is coincidental.

© 2004 by Michael Cowl Gordon. All rights reserved.

No part of this book may be reproduced, stored in a retrieval system, or transmitted by any means, electronic, mechanical, photocopying, recording, or otherwise, without written permission from the author.

First published by AuthorHouse 06/11/04

ISBN: 1-4184-6255-1 (ebook)
ISBN: 1-4184-4727-7 (Paperback)

Library of Congress Control Number: 2003097671

Printed in the United States of America
Bloomington, IN

This book is printed on acid free paper.

Acknowledgments

No real autobiography of a cat would contain an acknowledgment page, given the natural sense of entitlement of those of the feline persuasion. So you, the reader, have found me out already. But I make no apology for this minor subterfuge. I had a story to tell, and there was no way to tell it that would be equal to the viewpoint of the family cat. The imperative to tell this tale came out of my grief over the death of my beloved wife, Gena "Penny" Browder Gordon in 1992. There was no thought at the outset to write a story for publication, but only the idea of the advancement of my own healing, as part of my own journey. I could never have predicted that my journalling would have developed into a book, nor would it have but for the encouragement of many fine people.

Most particularly, I want to thank my wife, Judy Linton Gordon, whose generous and loving spirit fills my life, and who has provided me with all the support and encouragement I needed to carry this project to its conclusion. My daughter, Michelle Yvonne Gordon, has been a joy to me beyond anything I could have imagined out of parenthood. She also has encouraged me every step of the way. Several friends and family members read the manuscript as it developed, and encouraged me to publish it. These dear people include Richard Abrohams, Al and Suzanne Mercer, Ellis Henson, Frances Somerville, Michael Clancy, Michael McGarry, Richard Schellman, Don Balduc, Dan and Anne Marie Dougherty, Chuck Moon, Chris Doyle, Ken Weiss, Nancy Rose, Rosemary Svela, Joy Madden, Oscar Grant, my niece, Ariela Shaag, my mother-in-law, Floy Linton, my mother, Bernice Cowl Gordon, and my brother-in-law, Joe Browder. Tom Scott offered valuable suggestions and criticisms as well as much positive energy. A special thank you goes to another brother-in-law, Greg Linton, and his wife, Amy, for allowing their cat, Bailey, to grace the cover of this book. The cats of the Gordon household will be impossible to live with if I fail to give them special mention, so thanks to Baby Blue, Smoogie, Lucy Locket, and Tiger. I couldn't have done it without you. And how could I fail to honor the original Black Jack, the inspiration for the story's narrator? Alas, he is no longer with us, having gone on to the spirit world in 1999. We also lost Archie in 2002, and miss him dearly. Chan Glazman must be thanked for his technical support. It is because of his efforts that I can be found at www.georgiacat.com. Please visit the website, where you will find, among other things, pictures of all the cats. If this story reaches a large audience, as I do hope that it does, it will not because of my efforts, but rather because of many people, known and unknown to me, who believe in its message. I thank you all. I do wish I had the space to name everyone who has been or will be a part of this experience.

The ideas expressed in the story are strictly those of the cat. However, as his Muse, I have drawn on many sources of inspiration. I have learned more than I could ever possibly comprehend from the wonderful people and animals I have met throughout the course of my life, whether they have been my patients, friends, family members, whether in the churches, synagogues, sweat lodges, or the 12-step rooms I have been privileged to attend. The writers of sacred texts are owed an inexpressible debt of gratitude, and many others have taught me much about spiritual matters, most particularly Joseph Campbell, Abraham Joshua Heschel, and Bill Wilson.

Music has enriched my life, and I have tried to fill these pages with the energy of sacred music. I want to thank all those who have devoted their lives to bringing the spirit in the form of music to the rest of us. Special thanks is offered for permission to use the following texts in this story:

Precious Lord, Take My Hand
Words and Music by Thomas A. Dorsey
Copyright © 1938 by Unichappell Music Inc.
Copyright Renewed
International Copyright Secured. All Rights Reserved

Go Down Moses
Words and Music by Fela Sowande
Copyright © 1955 by Chappell Co
Copyright Renewed
International Copyright Secured. All Rights Reserved

Poor little Jesus
Arranged by Ronnie Gilbert, Lee Hays, Fred Hellerman, Pete Seeger
TRO- © Copyright 1951 (Renewed), 1952 (Renewed)
Folkways Music Publishers, Inc.
New York, New York
Used by Permission

Most importantly, I want to thank my Creator for making this wonderful world, placing me in it, loving me continuously, and for teaching me as is expressed in Lakota, *mitakuye oyesin*, we are all related.

Michael Cowl Gordon
January 24,2004
Marietta, Georgia

For Penny

1

What a friend we have in Jesus,
All our sins and grief to bear;
What a privilege to carry
Everything to God in prayer.

I never knew who my father was. It was mother who taught us how to hunt and fish. There were seven of us, four boys and three girls, raised under an old shed in a railroad yard. None of this is unusual for a cat. I didn't look like any of the others; two of the boys were orange tiger-striped kittens; one of the girls was solid gray and long-haired; one boy and one girl were tortoise shell like mom; my other sister was white with gray markings; and I am black with a white tuxedo front, white paws and whiskers, and a tiny white mark at the right corner of my mouth. Life was good in the railroad yard, every day bringing new adventures. Sometimes it was very noisy. The days were hot, and the evenings didn't cool off that much in the Georgia summer; but we were young and didn't really know hot from not back then. As we got a little older mom would let us go out and explore. All the new smells, sights, and sounds made life exciting and wonderful. We played with each other, wrestling and mock hunting games, hide and seek, and mom fussed over us mightily. One day a man discovered us and brought mom some milk and cat food. She always dragged us back inside if people came near, and actually moved us a couple of times. She would scold me and tell me I was the nosiest kitten she ever heard of. Then she would wash me with her rough tongue, and I knew she wasn't mad at me. I've since learned that people fuss at each other too, often affectionately. Cora was like that, but she could be mean too. But I'm getting ahead of myself.

As we got bigger mom started to wean us, and introduced us to solid food, mostly small rodents which God provided for us in abundance, but we also had an occasional snake or bird. She showed us how to hunt and prepare critters to eat. These experiences used to fill me with a kind of wild excitement, the intensity of which has never been duplicated in my lifetime. I think the very act of learning is uniquely exciting and wonderful; and of course, during kittenhood everything is new.

We grew rapidly. As time progressed we were allowed to wander away from the nest and explore the world on our own. I was never afraid of people, so I would instinctively approach the areas where the men worked. There was some danger from trains, but in the yard they moved slowly and made so much noise that it was easy to avoid them. I did have one terrifying episode though. I had been sunning myself on the ground next to a locomotive that was standing by itself on a siding. It was hot in the mid-afternoon sun, so I crawled under the train for some relief, and dozed off. The next thing I knew, there was a terrific racket. An incredibly loud hissing noise assaulted my left ear, and the train started to move. Everything happened so fast there was no time to think. My first reaction was to freeze. Less than a second later I was ready to bolt, but the train was already moving, and I froze again until it was gone. When I got home I was still visibly shaken. I told mom and the others what had happened. She was sweet and gave me a good washing, all the time lecturing us about the dangers of trains and the importance of minding her when she warns us about things. She said there was another kind of thing called a car that was even more dangerous because you might not see it coming until it was too late. She took us over to a road which ran by the yard and told us that it was the kind of track that cars ran on; and of course, never to cross it unless she was there to help us. I must confess that the fright of my experience left me quickly, and I have spent a lifetime crossing streets as well as railroad tracks with not so much as another close call. But I realize I've been lucky. I have seen many a broken and bruised cat through the years that were not so fortunate as I. I suppose it has been God's will that I have survived to this point, and I thank Him daily, as all cats do.

One day when I was around nine or ten weeks old, I left home for good without planning to do so. It had drizzled all morning, and I had been out and about chasing critters of one sort or another, pretty much oblivious to the weather. After a while I entered an old shed where I encountered a man who also was taking refuge from what had turned into a steady downpour. He picked me up and started stroking my fur, telling me how pitiful I looked. He smelled of sweat and stale whiskey, an aroma with which I later became well acquainted; but he was very nice, as most people are. I quickly explored the small shed, and then curled up on his lap for a snooze. Suddenly I was awakened by a jolt as he had gotten up and was running along side of a slowly moving train, carrying me along with him. Before I could collect my little cat thoughts, I had been tossed into an open boxcar, and he had jumped in next to me. What a rush! The car was empty, except for us of course, and I was torn between the urge to explore it, and my fascination with watching the world move outside. I managed both tasks quite nicely, as it developed that I had plenty of time. My companion had hidden himself in a corner and gone to sleep, and after I had sufficiently explored that little piece of the world, I joined him.

It was late afternoon when I awakened. The train was stopping, my hobo-pal had picked me up again, and before the train had quite stopped, he (we) jumped off, staggered a bit, and started walking along the tracks towards town. He didn't put me down until we arrived at the town square where I encountered no end of new and wonderful things to investigate. My excitement was somewhat tempered by the nagging hunger in my belly, so I started looking around for mom. It didn't take long for my wonder and amazement to turn to terror as I realized that I was lost, and not only could I not find my way home, but I couldn't find my new pal either. I spent a terrible night roaming around the town square, nearly getting killed by tomcats on two different occasions. That was the night that I realized that people are much nicer than other cats, by and large. I encountered a few mice but wasn't skilled enough at that time to catch one. I discovered garbage, but nothing that tasted good, and by morning I truly was a pitiful kitten. My face and left shoulder were sore where one of the toms had clawed and bitten me, I was awfully hungry and weak, and as it had rained half the night I was soaked once again. Earlier in the evening I had encountered my traveling companion asleep on a bench and smelling much more strongly of whiskey. I had been unable to arouse him, and when I came by that way later on he was gone. I never did see him again. I suppose one could criticize what he had done to me, but I think he acted out of loneliness and I bear no resentment. After all he is also one of God's creatures, and none of us are perfect. I would have had to set out on my own pretty soon anyway,

3

and would never have had the wonderful life I did have had he not brought me to Marietta.

By daylight I had crossed the railroad tracks that ran back of some buildings which fronted the square, and drawn by the aroma of food cooking, found myself huddled next to the dumpster behind a fried chicken place. Men were gathering in the parking lot, quietly talking and drinking coffee. Every once in a while a man would drive up in a pick-up truck, some of the others would jump in the back, and they would drive off. Other men would drive up in their cars and go inside for a while. Finally it stopped raining, and I timidly crawled out of my partially sheltered hiding place. Some papers which smelled of food were strewn about, but what cat can live on fumes? There were quite a few birds also, but I couldn't have caught one at that age even if I had been well rested and fed. Two men had left the fried chicken place and were saying a few parting words to each other standing next to a car. I felt drawn to them, and started rubbing my face and flanks on their legs.

This simple, instinctive act determined the course of the rest of my life, in accordance with God's divine plan. In the beginning when He created the world and made the cat in His own image, in His infinite wisdom He created man to be the perpetual guardian of His beloved creatures. He instilled both cat and man with instincts so that His divine will would be carried out. Cats, and more particularly kittens, appear extremely adorable to humans. They love the way we purr, wash ourselves, and roll over and look at them upside-down. They love our adorable little faces with our cute little ears, noses, whiskers, and sharp little kitty teeth. We are given the wiles to capture them in our feline webs with the result, in the ideal world, that we are perpetually cared for and provided with every comfort. So without realizing it, I was the instigator in a drama which has been played over and over for many thousands of years. As I rubbed up against these men, one of them picked me up, cradled me in his arms, and started talking to me, mostly just saying "Po' thing, po' thing, po' thing." Thus did I meet Archie, and for many years we were inseparable.

He wrapped me in his jacket, got in the car, and off we went. We stopped briefly, and he left me in the car for a moment, but not long enough for me to become anxious. A few minutes later we stopped again. This time he carried me, still wrapped up, into a house where he lived with Cora and Mama. He brought me into the kitchen and quickly produced a small

4

bowl of cold milk for me. After letting me remedy my half-starved state he wrapped me up in the jacket again. As we walked to the front of the house we encountered Cora.

"What you got there?" she demanded.

"Nuthin," he mumbled. I soon learned that one of his techniques for dealing with Cora was to mumble so that she couldn't understand what he was saying. This allowed him to reply without really replying, to irritate her, and to say vicious and ugly things to her without her being sure that he had insulted her.

Quickly foiling his evasion, I poked my little face out to satisfy my curiosity, and there she was. What struck me first was her eyes, which appeared to be popping out of her face directly at me. I dove back inside the jacket, having seen all I needed to at that moment.

"Don't you bring no cat in here around my mama!" she exclaimed.

"Mumble, mumble, mumble."

They proceeded to fuss for a while, Archie carrying me back and forth, keeping himself between Cora and me. Before too long there was a new development which took the heat off of me (but not poor Archie).

"What's this?" Cora grabbed a pint bottle out of his jacket pocket. "Don't you bring no whiskey into my mama's house you heathen!" She headed back to the kitchen with Archie (and me) close behind. Archie quickly put me down to rescue his bottle, but it was too late. Down the drain it went. I scurried away and left them to exchange verbal blows, Archie now articulating his words much more clearly.

Now that Cora and Archie were fully occupied, I was free to explore. This was my first time in a human's residence, so all the smells, objects, and little places held my fascination for a few seconds at a time. I wandered in and out of Mama's room briefly, and we regarded each other curiously, but I had too much investigating to do to stay very long. And before long I had ducked behind a chair in the living room and fallen asleep.

Well, somehow they worked things out. As our lives went on together I came to see that even though Cora was twice Archie's size, talked very tough, and had a frighteningly quick and hot temper, Archie got his way most of the time. Having whiskey in the house wasn't really a problem as long as Cora didn't see him drink it. His habit was to go to his room, close the door, turn on the TV, and quietly sip his Jim Beam. I could never see much effect that it had on him, at least not until the last couple of years of his drinking. And clearly I had a home. It was not without conflict, and at times I appeared to be at the center of it, but who expects life to go smoothly all the time?

I grew quickly, and soon was jumping up on things. This turned out to be not always good. There were certain locations that were declared off limits by either Cora or Mama. There was a white sofa in the living room that was perfectly suited as my main resting place, my black fur contrasting with it so beautifully. I was shooed off of it several times per day, and it got so that the vacuum cleaner stayed right there so that the traces of my sleek blackness could be quickly removed. The kitchen counter seemed to be a place of kitty unwelcomeness, and disapproval was expressed when I took a refreshing drink out of the toilet. However, none of these transgressions evoked anything like the reaction when I would jump up on Mama's bed. The first time I did it Mama was napping, and I decided to help her by keeping her company. I curled up on the pillow right next to her face, assuming that was what it was there for. After a pleasant while Mama stirred, and sleepily opened her eyes, staring into mine no more than two inches away. She was not pleased, and gave out a shriek that sent me flying out of the room. Cora came after me with a broom and a vengeance, and probably would have really hurt me had not Archie opened the back door to let me escape. Later I heard Mama explain to a friend on the telephone that I had been stealing her air. This is but one example of the numerous absurdities which people have come to believe about cats. If only God had made people a little smarter, many of the evils in the world could have been avoided.

The truth of the matter is once Mama got used to me she liked me, and so for that matter, did Cora. When Mama was sitting in her chair I would jump in her lap. She would stroke me and talk to me real sweetly, telling me all kinds of stories about the old times. I loved these stories, about her mama, about the house where she grew up in Cordele, and about her childhood. She talked about going to church on Sundays, her starched dresses, the wonderful preaching and singing of hymns; and she told me about Jesus. Sometimes she would even sing to me, a song about Jesus, softly stroking my fur, rubbing me gently, feeling me purr. Initially, Cora came to like me because Mama liked me. Cora had a little more time to herself when I was keeping Mama occupied. But although she was slow to admit it, she responded to her own natural God-given instincts to like and to want to care for cats. She gradually came to appreciate me for the charming and handsome feline that I was. Her scolding came to be habitual good-natured banter rather than out of anger. She was, in truth, a sweet and very bright, sensitive woman when she wasn't feeling threatened.

My territory extended to the outside world as well. We lived in a neighborhood of small, tidy bungalows with well-kept yards. In the spring and summer especially, the flowers were beautiful, and people were busy during the day trimming their shrubs, mowing their lawns, and so on. Sometimes people cooked outdoors, producing lovely aromas of meat simmering on the grill. Most of them enjoyed my visits, and were kind, petting and talking to me. I went by the name of Black Jack, which Archie had given me, and most everybody around there knew and liked Black Jack. As I matured I enjoyed going out at night. I felt strong stirrings within me, and was drawn to females in heat. This could lead at times to fights with the other toms, which I admit I didn't shy away from. I was bigger than average and could hold my own against most any tom in the neighborhood. Archie used to brag about what a good fighter I was.

And so I had a life. Things at home were not perfect, but the problems seemed manageable. I enjoyed my prowlings, and very much enjoyed hunting. Occasionally I would eat a mouse if I was hungry, but usually brought my little trophies home for Archie to admire. I would bring home mice, voles, moles, chipmunks, little rabbits, snakes and squirrels, and occasionally a bird or a lizard. Archie always had high praise for me and told me what I fine cat I was, even though he never seemed to want to actually eat my offerings. I was always careful to leave them outside, especially after the time when I left a snake that was still squirming in the kitchen, and Cora had one of her more memorable explosions.

And I began to meditate. This actually started when I still lived in the rail yard with mother. I would see her sit quietly, staring directly ahead, purring sometimes, seemingly deep in thought. I asked her later what she was doing, and she said she was feeling God's presence, and that I too would soon have this experience. And so I did. I have come to understand that the act of meditation is the highest purpose in the life of a cat. Such inner contact with our Creator gives a sense of bliss, sometimes approaching ecstasy. C.S. Lewis used the word "Joy" to describe it, and I don't have a better one. But then, why should I? Words are what people are best at. I began to meditate several times daily when I reached maturity. Gradually my meditations took me to strange places. Some cats say that the soul of a cat passes through several incarnations, and that these images represent memories from previous lifetimes. Each incarnation is a step in the purification of the soul, leading it towards its ultimate objective of oneness with God. I must say that I have loved my life: the wonderful people I have known, the hunting, the feral interaction with other cats, the music I have been blessed to hear, and the knowledge and wisdom I have gained. These have all been part of my life, and without them there would have been no life; and they all have been part of the spiritual journey towards union with the Creator, as most intimately experienced in this lifetime in the act of meditation.

This appears to be one of the differences between cats and people. Maybe people are handicapped by the fact that they do have language. It has been my observation that what comes naturally to a cat often leaves people without a clue. Mama is the most spiritual person I have known, but most of her relating to God was her talking to Him. I know she didn't hear Him nearly as clearly as I do. If she had, she wouldn't have been so frightened about leaving this world and moving on to the next.

2

Just a closer walk with Thee,
Grant it Jesus, is my plea.
Daily walking close to Thee,
Let it be, dear Lord, let it be.

I mentioned before that Archie liked to watch TV. Mama and Cora had a TV in the back of the house that they watched occasionally. I don't think Cora ever watched it except to keep Mama company. Mama mostly listened to the radio. She had an old model with crackly reception. I used to find this grating on my nerves until I became accustomed to it, like so many other things in life. The radio was on most of the time, always to the same station. In fact it was many years later that I discovered one could get more than one station on a radio. Mama liked to listen to gospel radio. Most of the programming was music, but Sundays brought the preaching too. I enjoyed the music immensely, but usually found something else to do on Sunday. A major step in the development of my relationship with Mama was when she discovered that I liked the religious music. It was Cora who pointed it out to her. She noticed that I would invariably appear in their room whenever a James Cleveland song was on. I was also very fond of the Chicago Community Choir, but truthfully, it was all wonderful. I think everyone has his favorites. Once Mama realized that I liked her music, my stock went sky high. I was now allowed on the foot of her bed, and together we would listen to the brothers and sisters rock and roll in praise of Jesus. Sometimes she would hum along some of the old time tunes, or even sing a few bars in her screechy old-lady voice. Some of the songs brought a faint smile to her lips and a far-away look in her eyes, tears slowly trickling down her cheeks. Her favorite song was "The Old Rugged Cross." There was a piano in the family room, and Mama used to beg Cora to play it for her and sing "The Old Rugged Cross," but Cora never would. She was extremely self-conscious, and had the most complicated relationship with God of anyone I ever knew. She just couldn't bring herself to do it. The only person I ever heard play that piano was Lexie, who always said it was out of tune. After Lexie died Mama couldn't even look at the piano, let alone ask Cora to play it.

So the radio was my electronic access to spirituality, but the TV was my electronic access to the rest of the world. For a long time I would just sit with Archie and watch what he watched. This would hold my interest for only a few minutes at a time, largely because he watched boring old shows like "Father Knows Best" and "Ozzie and Harriet." But Archie had a magical device in his room that opened the whole world to me, and changed my life. That device was what he referred to as "the remote." I have since become computer literate, which has given me the power to express ideas as well as learn them, but it was the TV as made accessible by the remote that opened the door to knowledge.

I had noticed how Archie would turn the TV on and off and change channels with the remote, but never gave it that much thought. One day he had gone out and left the TV on. I jumped onto his chair and curled up to a tedious episode of "Wagon Train" when I rested my paw on the remote, and suddenly, no Ward Bond. I kept pressing the same button, and the station kept changing. I tried different buttons. Pretty soon I had found the volume control, and was cranking pretty good when in charged Cora, her eyes stretching, my cue to a quick exit. Later she told Archie what had happened and scolded him about leaving the TV on when he leaves the house. He gave this the consideration that he customarily gave her admonishments. However, the cat was out of the bag, so to speak. It didn't take me any time at all to learn how to turn the TV on and off. Sometimes I would get careless and run up the volume, and Cora would come and put up the remote where I couldn't get at it. It wasn't long before this odd behavior of mine was taken for granted by the family even though Cora was vaguely troubled that I might have been possessed by a demon. Mama set her mind at rest about that, pointing out that sometimes I watched the Christian station (though not very often, as the music was bad, the preaching worse, and the people very peculiar). Mostly, I watched public TV or the Discovery Channel. The big deal for me was Sesame Street, because it was by watching this show that

10

I learned to read. I learned to count too, although this had little practical value. There is a tom down the street named Hemingway who has extra toes on his fore paws. This fact is of passing interest to me as a neighbor. The fact that he has specifically two more toes on his paws than anyone else is of no interest whatsoever to a cat. But learning to read was the biggest deal ever, although I didn't put this to any practical value until I gained access to a computer and that wonder of wonders, the Internet.

So I had discovered a new source of knowledge, and a vast one at that. This in addition to learning from nature, from other cats, from people, and from meditation. As I loaded my little cat brain up I would sometimes speak of things or make suggestions that gave me a reputation as quite an eccentric among my feline peers. Like the time, for example, when I suggested the neighborhood cats get together and put on a production of "My Fair Lady". I wanted to cast Mister Whiskers as Alfred Doolittle and Goodnight Smith as Liza Doolittle. I, of course, was to be Henry Higgins. They just stared at me and walked away. So I learned to keep my worlds separate.

Life settled into a comfortable routine. During the day Cora cooked, cleaned, and cared for Mama. Mama would awaken late in the morning, and after Cora had bathed her, gotten her in a fresh gown, and done her hair, she would get her up and out of the bed. Mama walked very slowly and used a walker that I occasionally got tangled in as she bumped along, getting her and Cora most upset. What didn't work out too well either was walking up behind one of them and rubbing myself against the backs of their legs. It was very hard for me to remember to not do this, the behavior is so instinctive, but their reactions were so extreme that I learned to stop myself most of the time. Once Mama lost her balance, she was so startled, and fell backwards. Luckily, she fell against her bed which partially broke her fall. Cora warned her that she would break a hip if she wasn't more careful, Archie was blamed for it, and I was banished from her room for a few days. But back to the daily routine. After Mama had her breakfast she would watch a little TV, and then get back into bed or sit in her overstuffed chair at the foot of the bed and listen to the radio. The phone rang often, and she loved to talk with her friends.

Archie would get up early in the morning and drive over to the fried chicken place to meet his friends for coffee. Usually, he would take me with him, and let me check out the parking lot, chase the pigeons, and rub up against the men who waited there for work. He would then stop at the package store for his Jim Beam, come home, and read the paper. At some time during the morning I had to make my rounds, and make sure that everything in the neighborhood was as it should be. I also managed to find time for a couple of good naps. I had my favorite places where I liked to hang out, the chaise lounge on the front porch probably tops on the list. It was in the shade, there was usually a light breeze, and I had a great view of what was going on. Some time before lunch Archie would put out fresh water and cat food for me on the back porch. He also kept a watchful eye on my litter box that I used occasionally if I got stuck inside and couldn't get out. Cora fixed lunch and dinner for the three of them.

After lunch Archie was sent to the store with a list from Cora, and probably ran other errands. I didn't make the afternoon run, so I can't say exactly what he did.. Mama took a nap after lunch, sometimes with my assistance. Cora would get busy with the laundry and some cleaning, and sometimes read or doze herself. Later on after Archie returned, she would start dinner. He went to his room at the front of the house, turned on the TV, and nodded in his chair. The five o'clock local news was his signal to start sipping on the Jim Beam, but he was still in good shape at dinner time. After dinner, he did the dishes, and retired to his room for an evening of quiet inebriation, game shows, and old Westerns and sitcoms. Mama and Cora would visit, watch TV, or talk on the phone. Mama kept Cora busy with many projects of one sort or another. Mama was active in her church where she had been a member since God was a Little Boy. She remained on numerous committees, and was forever on the phone asking people for money for one project or another. Cora got stuck with most of the work though, and she didn't even go to church. Her reasons were complicated, but I think the main one was that she was self-conscious because of her weight.

Archie was always the first one to go to bed. He would let me out around nine to do my feline thing. Cora and Mama stayed in the back of the house, and if I wanted to get back in, I would go to the back door and scratch at it until Cora let me in. Once the lights were out, usually between one and two A.M., I could forget about getting back in. This was fine because it was prime hunting time, and I had to have my fun. If the weather got bad, once I had caught my prey, I would stay under the house until Archie got up.

Sundays were different. For one thing, Archie didn't stop at the package store, because it was closed. He would always get two pints on Saturday. But the main difference was that Mama went to church. This was a major production. Cora got Mama up early. They both moved pretty slowly, so it took a long time to get Mama sufficiently presentable. Lexie would come over around ten and fix Mama's make-up and hair. Mama eventually took to wearing a wig, but getting it right was no simple operation either. All morning the crackly radio belted forth singing and preaching. Lexie always brought her little girl, Emily, and once in a while Lenny, her husband, would come.

This gets me to an issue I need to comment on. People are strange. At the beginning of the story I described myself, and my brothers and sisters according to our color and markings. The only purpose was to be descriptive, and to convey a visual image to the reader to add to the enjoyment of the story. It seems that people attach importance to individual differences in color and markings in their kind that cats would never dream of doing. People would sometimes come over to visit Mama and I would hear an occasional reference to "that white man that Lexie is married to." Cora and Mama always came to her defense and said that not only was Lenny very nice, but that he was very good to Lexie and the baby, and a better husband than a lot of black men they knew. Cora would on occasion get very angry and have personal things to say about the "no good niggers" that some of them were married to. These conversations didn't always end harmoniously, and Mama would be so mortified that she would practically be in tears, and afterwards would beg Cora not to talk that way to her friends. Cora would blaze with anger, and not back down. She was very fond of Lenny, and wasn't going to let anyone talk badly about him. Most of the time these episodes would blow over, and the people would come back another time and visit just as pleasantly as if nothing had ever happened. Once Mama backed Cora up when some lady said something about Lexie's "half-white baby." Cora actually pushed her out the door, and she never came back. As I have said, she had a terrible temper, but in this case she was right, and I kind of got a kick out of it.

Sunday became my favorite day because of Emily. She was a very little person, the smallest I had ever seen. I have since learned that people take about twenty times as long as cats to mature and become self-sufficient (and even worse, some never do). Emily was about three years old, and she adored me. She got down on the floor with me and did annoying little things like pull my tail and stick her fingers in my ears, and tried to dress me up in her clothes. I have a tolerant disposition and was able to deal with this better than most cats; and as a result, we became very close. Emily certainly found me more interesting than anyone or anything else in the household, if I can say so. I didn't even mind sharing my food and water with her, but Lexie caught us at it one day, and had enough to say about it, and with sufficient feeling, that Emily got the point. Now that I think about it, Lexie had a little bit of Cora's fire in her, even though, as I eventually learned, she wasn't Cora's daughter.

Mama and Papa Porter had four children who survived to adulthood. Cora was the oldest. Next was Constance, who was Lexie's mother. Constance had already died, as had Lexie's father, Jack Dobbins, both because of what they referred to as "sugar." Lexie also had a younger brother Jake who had been killed in a crack house several years earlier. This had thrown the whole family into a severe depression and was said to have contributed to Jack and Constance dying so young. By the time I joined the family, they had gone through their grieving, but clearly Mama would never really get over her loss of her daughter and grandson. Mama also had a younger son and daughter whom I rarely saw because they lived up North in Ohio.

After church Cora would serve a big dinner, and always got complemented on how excellent it was. The highlight for me was getting a taste of the homemade ice cream she made every Sunday. Lenny was more likely to come for dinner than for church, as he usually played golf on Sunday mornings. Besides, he was Jewish, so he went to a different church. One day I learned that Jesus had been Jewish, so I guess he would have gone to Lenny's church too. People's religions can be awfully confusing, and I have heard some heated arguments between members of different faiths, and even worse arguments among members of the same faith. It is ironic that the harder some people try to approach God, the further away they sometimes get. When the primary motivator for religious belief is fear (of death mostly) then people can get rigid, judgmental, and intolerant. But when they begin to get a hint of the oneness of all things, the attraction to God comes from that inner awareness of God's love. I wish people would listen to less preaching about Hell, and learn to meditate. I realize that the world is going to evolve towards a higher spiritual plane at its own pace, but I do hate to see so much unnecessary confusion and suffering.

After Sunday dinner things would quiet down. Lenny, Lexie, and Emily would go home, Archie and Mama would retire to their rooms, and Cora would putter around the house. Sometimes people would drop in to visit after church, dressed in their finest clothes and looking grand. I always did like to see folks dress up, but some of those ladies did put the oddest things on their heads. Sunday afternoon for me was a good time to catch up on my napping.

I would also get out and check out the goings on in the neighborhood. I enjoyed having a private cat life that didn't involve the people I lived with. There were many other cats around. I wasn't too tight with many of them as cats can be rather aloof. My closest feline friend was Grits, a pretty gray and white female who lived two streets over from me. I called on her every day. She had a lovely disposition, was affectionate, liked to patrol with me, and was a good companion during quiet times. We would sometimes say our afternoon prayers together, and, of course, co-meditate. Another cat I got along with fairly well was Sampson, a huge tortoise-shell Maine Coon who lived sort of across and the down the street from me. He was as gentle as he was big, and had much wisdom and serenity about him. He was clearly in an advanced incarnation, a very spiritual cat. It was Sampson who explained to me the principle of duality. You know, earth and sky, male and female, sun and moon, good and evil, cat and dog. He explained the paradox of how this principle operates in a world in which a greater principle is the oneness of all things. The answer, he said, lies in another duality, appearance and reality. Our challenge is to be at peace with the world's intrinsic conflicts, even to appreciate them, and to never lose sight of the oneness of all things. The path to this Way is meditation, and to a lesser extent, prayer. Sampson helped me too with something that had always bothered me. Three times daily cats pray, and one of our prayers is thanking God for not having made us a dog. I had vague misgivings about denigrating one of God's creatures, even if it was the dog, in prayer. Sampson explained to me that the natural superiority of the cat to the dog was one of God's mysteries, and that the cat's gratitude for this is an aspect of the natural order of things, to be reverentially experienced, not questioned.

By this time the nights had become quite cool, and longer than they had been originally. At first I thought Archie was getting up earlier, but that wasn't it. I began to notice changed behavior in some of the little prey animals. They were storing food, some were growing longer coats,

15

and new birds were arriving. It was explained to me about the changing of the seasons being another of life's rhythms. Many creatures and plants depend on the changing of the seasons to procreate, although that wasn't particularly the case for more advanced animals such as cats or humans. Speaking of biological variation, did you know that the human female is the only species that is sexually receptive when she is not ready to conceive? Sampson's theory is that God made them that way because they mate with one partner for life, and it keeps the male from wandering to other females. I think he is mistaken, however, based on my own observations of human mating behavior.

One night Archie let me out before he went to bed, and I was shocked at how cold it was. It had rained earlier that day, and the remaining puddles of water had frozen solid! I cut my routine extremely short. Cora chuckled when she let me back in, and said something to me about my not being so interested in "doin' no tomcattin'" that night. As time went on, I got more used to the cold weather. Archie and Cora had once lived "up North" and would enjoy telling stories about how cold it got there. I have no idea how a cat could survive in that climate.

And so my life settled into its mostly pleasant routine. Things were familiar, predictable, natural, and comfortable. It was filled with good things in abundance, and it was easy to praise God. I was aware that bad things can happen, but since nothing bad had happened to me, I assumed that tragedy would always keep its distance. Actually, I don't think I ever really thought about it. I took my comfort and happiness for granted. But as we all learn sooner or later, nothing stays the same forever. What I thank God for today is that when the troubles came, He comforted me through my family, friends, and spiritual practices of prayer and meditation.

3

The river Jordan is deep and wide
Hallelujah!
Milk and honey on the other side
Hallelujah!

I was in my fourth summer. Nothing too radical had happened in my life, the changes being more subtle. Emily was noticeably bigger, and marginally less of a pest. Archie had taken to start drinking right after lunch and was buying two pints per day instead of one. Mama slept more, and didn't get around quite as well. Neither, for that matter, did Cora, who had taken to rubbing all sorts of evil-smelling liniments on her knees, and even used a walker at times. There was a new host of the morning gospel radio show, Brother Parker. Cora and Archie argued more about nothing in particular. Some Sundays Mama didn't go to church. But the changes were so gradual that things didn't seem all that different or problematic.

One morning that changed. I was making my rounds just before sunrise, and had entered a field I often enjoyed on my way to Grits' house. Usually it was a snap to catch a mouse in the tall grass there, but I had no luck that morning. I had just emerged from the field when I heard a soft whimpering sound coming from just across the street. I approached cautiously (how else would a cat approach?) and was horrified to find Grits lying in the street next to the curb. She was unable to move her hind legs, and appeared to be kind of out of it. Her coat was dirty, and I could smell blood. I sniffed at her and pushed at her with my forehead. She seemed to recognize me, but as I said, she was in shock. I didn't know what to do. I tried to give her a little wash but she complained, so I stopped. It was starting to get light, and every once in a while a car would go past. After what seemed like a very

17

long time a lady a couple of houses away came out to water her flowers and after a couple of minutes noticed that something was wrong. She came running over to see what the trouble was, and quickly went back into her house for a blanket. She carefully wrapped Grits in the blanket and brought her into the house. Soon, Grits' guardian came running in a panic and went into the house also. Then both ladies came out carrying Grits, got in a car, and drove away.

I crossed the streets a little more carefully on my way home as it was obvious that she had been hit by a car. I had gotten to where I never gave crossing the street a second thought. Either I was good at it or lucky, because I never had even a close brush with a car. Archie had already gone on his morning run, so Cora let me in. I moped around all day, worried about my friend, and didn't eat much. When I was outside I wanted to come in, and when I was inside I wanted to go out. Cora fussed at me and asked what was wrong. At dinnertime she told Archie that something was wrong with me, and maybe he should take me to Doctor Jeff tomorrow, but Archie was already half in the bag by then and only mumbled. So she fussed at him too. Later that evening, as I continued to mope, Mrs. James called Cora on the phone. It turns out this was the lady who found Grits. Of course, I didn't know who was on the phone but it was clear this was no ordinary conversation. Cora's eyes got big. Her part of the conversation was "my, my, my," "Lawd have mercy," and "mm, mm, mm," and to cast an alarmed glance at me from time to time. After she hung up she told Mama that Grits had been hit by a car. Mrs. Johnson and Mrs. James had taken her to the vet who said she had a broken pelvis and a broken tail. The tail wasn't much of a problem, but an operation to set the pelvis would cost a thousand dollars. Grits was spending the night at the vet while Mrs. Johnson decided what she was going to do.

"Mrs. Johnson don't got no thousand dollars to spend on no cat," Mama said. Then they talked about how maybe Grits would have to be "put to sleep." I couldn't have been more upset.

That night while on the prowl, I went back to where I had found Grits next to the curb. The smell of blood and fear lingered strongly and troubled me deeply. I discovered that night that it was a lot easier to be accepting and philosophical about life and death when it didn't affect me directly. I half-heartedly caught a mouse and brought it home for Archie. I didn't feel like going on the morning run, but did so mostly out of habit. I had

18

to force myself to say my morning prayers, and couldn't meditate at all. I had the first headache of my life. I was disturbed by the casual indifference most of the neighborhood cats had to Grits' plight, and couldn't even locate Sampson for some words of wisdom or consolation.

It was a long day. Every time the phone rang my ears stood straight up, hoping for news, yet fearing the news. Late that night Cora called Mrs. James and learned that Grits was still at the vet. At least she hadn't been put down yet, and this gave me some hope. I was finally able to meditate, and as a result, began to become aware of my selfishness in the situation. The tragedy would not be for Grits if she died, because death is part of the life cycle. She is on a path towards spiritual purification, as we all are. The loss would be mine because I had become dependent upon her companionship. I realized that I had to become willing to let her go, and to praise God for the natural order of His creation. These thoughts were of some slight comfort, but I remained acutely depressed. I spent another night of going through the motions of being a cat.

The next day brought a call from Mrs. James some time before noon. Mrs. Johnson had brought Grits home. She would keep her confined to a cage for six weeks. It was possible that the pelvis would heal without an operation if Grits could be kept from running and jumping. Doctor Jeff had prescribed a mild sedative to try to keep her quiet and relieve her pain for a few days. Time would tell.

I visited Grits every day. I would go to her house after the morning run and scratch at the front door until Mrs. Johnson let me in. They both enjoyed my visits, and Mrs. Johnson always had some little kitty treat for me, usually one of those frozen anchovies. It was painful to see Grits in a cage. She was pretty disgusted with her new life, but tried to make the best of it. We knew that she might still have to be put down, but never spoke of anything other than how wonderful it would be when she got well. I brought her the neighborhood news, we visited, and would always meditate together.

I'm sure that it was the critical nature of her situation that affected us so, because both of us experienced our meditations taking us places we had never been before. In one, I was in a terrible place where people were chained to each other in a small dark building. It was hot, with a strong odor of sweat, urine, and fear. One by one they were taken outside and made to stand on a platform. Men would walk up and inspect them, poke and prod at them, and in general be incredibly disrespectful. There was another man who seemed to be in charge who would call out in a sing-song voice, and make both complimentary and disparaging remarks about the person on the platform. Every so often, someone would give the auctioneer money, and then take the person on the platform away, still in chains.

Thus far in my tale, I have made no reference to beauty or relative attractiveness, or lack thereof, of the people I tell about. This is because I am telling the story from my own perspective; and from the point of view of a cat, the physical beauty of a person is not only irrelevant, but also based on arbitrary standards set by people, not cats. I have said that Grits is pretty because she is, and from my standpoint it adds to the story. I will now also tell you that according to all comments I have ever heard, Lexie was a strikingly beautiful woman. Her skin was perfect, features beautifully sculpted, her shape softly curved and feminine, and her smile was electrifying. It is also a well-known fact that some of the physical features that give people (or cats) their own distinctive appearance can be hereditary. So I had the strangest feeling when, in my vision, the next person brought out to the platform was a young girl probably between fourteen and sixteen years of age. Her eyes were large and dark, blazing with anger and fear. The resemblance to Lexie was striking, and I couldn't take my eyes off of her. The man raved about her beauty, and said she was strong and could bear fine children. From inside the shed a woman's voice could be heard wailing, but I couldn't make out what was said. The girl was disrobed so that her breasts were exposed. After much bidding a man bought her, put a rope around her neck, tied the other end to a horse, and led her away. She never said a word, nor did any of the slaves I saw sold that day. The vision faded and my attention returned to Grits in her cage. I was troubled and confused with what God had shown me, and kept it to myself for a long time.

One day while Grits was still in her cage awaiting her yet to be determined fate, Archie failed to come home from his afternoon run. I have already mentioned that he was up to two pints per day, and was now starting to drink right after lunch. Cora would fuss at him about going out and driving after drinking whiskey.

"You gonna kill somebody driving like that," she would say; or, "Don't call me to get you out of no jail if you get a DUI."

I didn't get what the problem was exactly, but words were exchanged about it on a daily basis. Every once in a while there would be a story on the news about someone getting killed by a drunk driver, or some celebrity or other getting a DUI. It appeared that cars could be just as dangerous to people or to other cars as they were to cats. And I guess I did have the notion that some people were more fit to drive than others. Cora had her own car, and occasionally went out driving. Mama would ask her not to, and cry and pray aloud to Jesus until she got back home. Then Mama would beg her to sell the car and stop driving because of her arthritis. I agreed with Mama on this, but thought she was even more unfit to drive because of her temper.

So Archie didn't show up for dinner, and Cora had her dander up about it. She stormed around the house muttering to herself about "that no-good nigger drinking that whiskey's gone and got himself killed or killed someone else!" She called several people and every emergency room in town. About eight Lexie called to tell her that Lenny had gone to bail him out of jail. He had run into the back of another car at an intersection, and was arrested for DUI. No one was hurt. It was almost midnight when they got home. As soon as Lenny had left, Cora lit into Archie. He retreated, mumbling, to his room and tried to close the door, but Cora was in his face and didn't let up. It was after two before she wound down. Mama spent the time crying and wringing her hands, calling out to Jesus. From time to time I went to the door and scratched, but everyone was too preoccupied to notice or to care that I wanted to get out of there.

The next day it was even worse. Everyone was irritable from lack of sleep, and Cora was enraged when Archie came home with his usual two pints. Mama was so upset she couldn't eat and she begged Cora to stop hollering. She called Lexie, who came over and got Cora out of the house for a while. Lexie was the only person who wasn't afraid of Cora when she got like that, and she seemed to have a calming effect on her even though she would get to hollering just about as bad as Cora. For some reason, when Lexie scolded her, she quieted down and listened. Lexie convinced her to settle down by telling her that if she didn't she would have a heart attack, and then nobody would be there to take care of Mama. So Cora let up on Archie for Mama's sake.

Actually, if Cora could not have cared for Mama, I'm sure Lexie would have, and Cora must have known that. But Cora needed to think that no one could take care of her Mama like she could, and she was probably right. She was very possessive of Mama, and wouldn't let anyone do much for her. When Mama's youngest daughter came from Ohio to visit, the fur would fly. Lulu would show up for several days, fix food for Mama that she wasn't supposed to eat, borrow money, talk on the phone to her sorority sisters, and generally stir up a hornet's nest. She would fuss over Mama, doing her hair, pampering her, and criticize how Cora did or didn't do this or that for Mama. She also made a big show of going to church with Mama, dressed to the nines. After she would leave, Mama would beg Cora to try to get along better with Lulu next time. Cora would fume and go through the silver and jewelry to see if anything was missing.

About a day after one of these visits Mama woke up in the middle of the night in a drenching sweat and couldn't catch her breath. I could hear the gurgling in her chest from the next room. Some men came and carried Mama out of the house on a cart and took her to a hospital. After a few days she was home and things got back to normal. Cora told Mama the doctor said she had eaten too much salt. Cora was always scrupulous about fixing low salt foods for Mama. She called Lulu and blamed her for Mama getting sick and almost passing. It was another ugly scene, and once again Mama cried and called upon Jesus to have mercy on her. Thereafter, Lulu's visits were more contentious than ever, and often followed by Mama having one of her spells and having to be rushed to the hospital. Lulu's position was that she was a nurse, she knew what was best for her mama, that Mama got sick because Cora got her so upset; and her timing was such that she always got out of town at least twelve hours before Mama had to be rushed to the hospital.

Have I mentioned fleas? One of God's mistakes, if you ask me. They are no problem in the winter, but the rest of the year they can make the life of a cat miserable. They jump up on you, have a delicious blood meal, and then jump off, leaving you to itch and scratch twenty-four and seven. And there is no getting away from them. I would scratch so much that I would leave blood all over the place, along with something Cora referred to as flea dirt. The first time this happened I left a little mess on Mama's bedspread. Not a good thing to do, Black Jack! So I next experienced the remedy for fleas, a cure worse than the disease. Cora grabbed me, plunged me into a metal washtub she kept in the back yard, and gave me a fierce scrubbing, muttering all the while about "not having no flea-infested cat" in her mama's house. Then she rinsed me off with the garden hose and wouldn't allow Archie to let me in until late that night after I had finally dried. She then insisted that Archie give me a weekly bath, which he did. Archie's baths were not so bad as Cora's, because he was not as passionate about the activity as she was, and he tried to keep the soap out of my eyes. Once I dried I was rewarded with a good brushing of my coat. I admit that most of the time the flea problem was kept tolerable with this approach. I had heard of flea powder and other less unpleasant remedies from other cats, and I wished for something like this for myself, but how could I convey my desires to Archie? I was stuck with the old-time way of doing things. I guess it wasn't really so bad. People frequently change how they do things in the interest of convenience or modernization, but this doesn't always make things any better. Quite the opposite, it often creates more problems, directly and indirectly. People can be so clever and so foolish at the same time.

I was saying that Archie got this DUI, and Lenny had gotten him out of jail. It turned out that this wasn't the end of it. He had to hire a lawyer and go to court. I had seen lawyers and courts on TV. Courts are places where smart lawyers get people out of trouble after they have been unfairly accused of something. My favorite lawyer was Perry Mason. You can imagine my surprise one day when I was watching TV and saw him push Jimmy Stewart out of a window. I guess anyone can have a bad day. There is another kind of court where people argue with each other and a judge decides who is right. I wasn't sure exactly which kind of court Archie had to go to, but what I am sure of is that it cost a lot of money. He complained about it all the time. Apparently, he had to pay the lawyer, and the judge made him pay a fine and something called court costs. Then he had to pay more money to go to what he called "DUI school." I never heard so much grumbling. Throughout it all he continued with his two-pint-a-day routine.

The day he went to court he put on a suit and tie just as if he was going to church. Luckily, it was in the morning, so he was sober, but I missed my visit to the fried chicken place. I hadn't realized that he owned a suit and tie up until then, as he never actually went to church. Well, he came home that afternoon, changed clothes, turned on the TV, opened his Jim Beam, and acted as though nothing had ever happened. One thing he did differently

23

from then on was to start buying it by the half-gallon. He said it was to save money. I think he did it to make sure he didn't run out. In that sense he was successful. He would buy two bottles at a time, and when he was on the last one he would buy two more. I can't say that he saved any money though. He started drinking a lot more, his hands started to shake in the morning, and he became more reclusive. He almost never left the house after lunch to avoid getting another DUI, and after a while he started drinking in the morning. This went on for a long while.

4

Jesus is the sweetest name I know,
and he's just the same as his lovely name;
that's the reason why I love him so.
Yes Jesus is the sweetest name I know.

When the six weeks were up Mrs. Johnson took Grits back to Doctor Jeff who said her pelvis had healed. She was allowed to hang out again like other cats. At first she was very weak because of her inactivity, but she quickly came back to her old self, except for her crooked tail. It bugged her, and she developed the disconcerting habit of chewing on it. Actually, she was slowly chewing it off, so Mrs. Johnson took her back to Doctor Jeff who amputated it, making everyone a lot happier. Grits and I had gotten closer through this episode, and we hung out together more from then on.

As Emily got older she was allowed to go out and play with me by herself, and we would take little walks together. She had other friends in the neighborhood that she would play with, and we would always go by and visit Grits together. Mrs. Johnson gave both of us a little milk and cookies, except that I always politely refused the cookies. I didn't care for all of Emily's friends. Some of them had dogs. While in principle, I have nothing against dogs, I do need to point out that they are stupid, hyperactive, slavering, noisy, and mean. So I would stay outside and poke around or nap while she did this visiting. It was hard to tolerate the odor of dog spit on her afterwards, but she was a good kid, and I tried to overlook her faults.

Archie gave her a little section of his garden to plant when she was six or seven, and she enjoyed this very much. She planted flowers, and when they bloomed she would immediately pick them and bring them in for Mama, and Cora would put them in a little vase. He showed her how to weed and cultivate, and gave her a little watering can made of green plastic.

She had a tendency to over-water, so Archie kept his eye on her. I enjoyed the garden as well. It was a fine place to sun myself, and as the yard was fenced in, I didn't have to worry about being bothered too much.

One day though, Emily and I were scared half to death out there. A stray dog wandered by, a big ugly thing with a yellow coat, and black lips and snout. He caught sight of me and was seized with the desire to bite me in two. The first thing I knew he was flying over the fence, eyes blazing, tongue flapping, saliva spraying every which way. I bolted, darting this way and that, feeling his hot horrible dog breath on me. Emily was hysterical, and in no time Lexie had her in the house. I shot up the pecan tree in the back yard just in time to save myself, while the miserable cur growled, snarled, and leaped at me. I found a limb safely out of his reach, and calmly stretched out, staring down at him contemptuously. I'm not proud of that, but I might as well tell it like it was. This went on for quite some time, with the added confusion of Archie coming outside with a big stick and yelling at the dog to go home. Finally, some men came and took the dog away, so it was safe to come down. Or was it? Now I wasn't so sure, and there was another thing. I had never been in a tree before, and wasn't sure how to get down. Lexie had come outside. She spoke to me nicely, telling me that it was safe to come down now. I stared at her. She reached up towards me, encouraging me to come down, but I was out of reach. Cora came out into the yard with some of my favorite snacks, calling to me. I climbed higher into the tree, this feeling more natural than climbing down.

Soon Archie reappeared, struggling with a ladder. Cora's eyes stretched as he positioned the ladder, and she told him he was going to fall and break his neck. She wanted to call the fire department but he was stubborn. Archie headed up the ladder more or less in my direction. For some reason, I found this alarming, I suppose because it was all so different from what I was used to. A lot of people are like this too. They become extremely uncomfortable with unfamiliar situations, and can act quite irrationally. Emily was like that when she was very little, and I noticed Mama getting that way at times. Anyway, as Archie got closer I climbed higher. He was alternatively talking nicely to me, muttering to himself, and cursing at me. The sight of him coming up towards me from below was unnerving, and felt like much more of a problem then being stuck in a pecan tree. So I kept safely out of reach. Suddenly he gave out with a holler. The ladder was starting to slip, and as Cora held on to it from below, Archie grabbed a branch, and together

26

they managed to steady it again. But now Archie was afraid to let go. Cora hollered for help, Lexie headed for the telephone, and then ran back outside to help Cora with the ladder. So there we were, and none of us having a very good time. Finally, I heard a siren, and pretty soon here comes the fire truck. Several men came with a much bigger ladder that they set up and helped Archie down. Then one of the men came after me. I tried to avoid him but eventually he got up to where I was. All I could do was bite and claw at him as he grabbed me and carried me down the ladder. Once down, I ran under the house. The fireman went inside so Cora could wash his face where I had left a nice claw mark. I later heard Archie say that it was a good thing he was able to find my rabies certificate. Cora must have put some medicine on his face too, because I could smell it later when I came in. Emily wouldn't go outside by herself for months after that episode.

One day while at the foot of Mama's bed and listening to the radio, I had another meditation in which it was nighttime and I was down by a riverbank, hunting. I came to a clearing where a few people had gathered, and more were arriving. Some of them had candles, but otherwise it was very dark. I heard drums in the distance. Soon there was quite a crowd of people, talking to each other very quietly, and some of them began to hum a tune I didn't know. More and more joined in, and one group started singing while others continued to hum. It was quite beautiful. Then a man began to preach. It was similar to what I heard on the radio, but then again, it wasn't. I found myself listening and caught up in the spirit of the gathering. He talked about freedom, and of Jesus and Moses. He mentioned the Pharaoh, about streets paved with gold, and about God and the children of Israel. I didn't follow the whole thing, but it was captivating in spirit. In the candlelight I recognized a woman as the girl I had seen sold as a slave in one of my previous meditations. She was a few years older, but it was definitely the same woman who looked like Lexie. There were more hymns, more preaching, and then a man who had been some distance away came and said there were horses coming. The candles were extinguished, and the people silently and quickly dispersed.

I emerged from the meditation to see Mama dozing in the bed and Cora dozing in her chair. Brother Parker was making public service announcements on the radio. Zion Baptist Church was having its 125th anniversary celebration at the church on Lemon Street this Sunday in Marietta. The children's choir would perform at four o'clock in the sanctuary. There would be arts and crafts for sale, and plenty of good food. Everyone was invited. Another church was having a revival in Decatur. The Church of God in Christ praised God for the arrival of their new pastor, Reverend Charles Williams, who had most recently served a church in Decatur, Alabama. The Atlanta Black Arts Festival would be in two weeks. There was a new exhibit on the history of Black churches in Georgia at the Atlanta History Society. Johnetta Cole, president of Spelman College, was to be the keynote speaker at next week's Black Leadership Conference.

I jumped off the bed and checked on Archie. He was starting to look poorly. His color wasn't good, and his arms and legs were looking more spindly. It seemed as though his abdomen was swollen, and there were dark circles under his eyes. I rubbed up against his legs as he sat in his chair. He was dozing too, but stirred, and picked me up in his lap. I jumped down, and went and scratched at the door until he got up and let me out. It was late autumn. Many of the flowers had faded or dropped, and the leaves were falling. It was cool, and the wind blew leaves about, along with some paper trash that seemed to be a constant part of the landscape. I felt the flow of things, the change of the seasons, the appearance and disappearance of cats and kittens, the drudgery of people's lives. My meditation had left me contemplative and a little melancholy. Powerful images were being presented to me but what did it all mean? I washed my face and said my prayers. The rest of that day was unremarkable.

Every once in a while Archie and I would stop by to visit Lexie. Usually she was the only one at home because Emily was at school, and Lenny was at work. I never fully understood what kind of a job he had, but I do know that his family owned a wholesale plumbing supply business, whatever that is. I was not allowed in the house proper, being confined to the back porch due to Lexie's allergy to cats, of all things. This might be another one of God's mistakes. After all, why should a guardian of His beloved creatures, whose primary purpose in life is to make the life of a cat pleasant and comfortable, be unable to be in the presence of a cat without getting sick? Actually, I jest when I refer to God's mistakes; there are no such things. But there certainly are things and circumstances in this world that we could do without. If there really were such a thing as the Devil, it would be a natural to blame allergy to cats on him.

Sometimes Archie would just visit for a few minutes and have coffee. Often, though, he would do some little job for her, like fixing a lamp or replacing a faucet. Evidently, Lenny didn't know how to do this kind of thing, and he took a fair amount of good-natured ribbing about it too. It was obvious that Archie enjoyed doing this for them, and I enjoyed the visits even though I wasn't allowed to come in. There were quite a few cats around there. Some of them were pretty friendly, but you always get the sort that acts as though they own their little piece of the world. I always get an attitude over that sort of thing. There is no cat I ever met who could back me down, and I enjoy a good fight once in a while. Some of the people over there didn't like me fighting with their cats, but that's okay too.

They had a nice house, quite a bit larger than Mama's. Every once in a while I would slip past Lexie and explore the many wonderful little places in it. When Emily was home sometimes she would sneak me in as well. Eventually I would be discovered and Lexie would shoo me out with much good-natured scolding. I also noticed that Archie would sometimes help himself to some of Lenny's whiskey while he was working around the house. Lexie usually had something she had baked for him, and milk for me. Once or twice a year Archie, Cora, and Mama all went over to Lexie's house for dinner, but they never brought me along on those occasions; and as time went on, it was harder and harder to get Mama out of the house, even for church. I think the last time Mama ever went over there was for her 95th birthday party. I think that's about eighteen in cat years. Everyone made quite a fuss about it, and she enjoyed the attention as she always did.

Cora was after Archie more and more to go to the doctor because he was looking worse and worse. Naturally, he would refuse, and always had some lame excuse. He did a lot of throwing up in the morning. Cats do that all the time and it's no big deal, but in his case it was obvious that he was sick. It was equally obvious that he wouldn't go to the doctor for fear that he would have to give up his whiskey. Doctors always do that sort of thing. Whether you are a person or a cat, if you get sick the doctor is likely to blame you for it, saying you eat too much of this or that delicious and wonderful substance (salt, grease, chocolate, squirrel), and prescribe some foul-tasting medicine.

Sometimes they demand that you perform some hideous ritual, like bathing in medicated shampoo or getting your teeth brushed. Luckily for me, while Archie was good at taking me for my shots every year, and even spent the extra money for the feline leukemia vaccine, he never took Doctor Jeff's advice too seriously. When I turned seven Doctor Jeff recommended he switch me to "light" cat food. I'd like to see him try and eat that stuff. I just picked at my food and acted so pitiful that Archie quickly switched me back to the real thing.

Well, one morning Archie got really sick. He was up earlier than usual, throwing up longer than usual, and not coming out of the bathroom. Cora eventually went to check on him, and immediately headed for the telephone to call an ambulance. I went to see for myself, being curious as a cat. Archie was on the floor next to the commode, pale as a ghost. He was covered with perspiration, and his eyes were glassy. His aim hadn't been that great, and there was quite a lot of blood around. The smell of blood and sickness was powerful. I rubbed against him but he was out of it and didn't respond. Cora was in a stew, pacing back and forth and saying words to the effect that she had warned him that something like this would happen. She washed his face with a cold cloth, and started cleaning the commode and floor. Pretty soon some men came and took Archie away on a cart, just like they always did Mama.

He was gone several days. We all worried a lot about him. I spent considerable time on the bed with Mama, listening to the radio, or to her little sermons. Mama had started preaching, and it didn't seem to matter too much to her if there was anyone there to listen or not. I always listened politely. She talked about how hard life is and how we have to put our trust in God who has a plan for us. Only God knows what is good and right for us so we don't question what happens. She had a favorite Bible passage, the one that starts "The Lord is my Shepherd, I shall not want…" which she recited frequently when she was troubled. Clearly, it comforted her, and I rather liked it myself. I didn't agree with her idea that God has a plan that includes this or that specific agony. To listen to her one would think that God takes our loved ones away from us or inflicts some other suffering upon us for some specific purpose known only to Him. And that somehow it is all to our benefit either in this world or in the next. I can't quite accept that. My journey has brought me to the understanding that suffering and loss are part of life. While God doesn't plan it out or cause it, neither does

He necessarily intervene or prevent all of it either. What God does do is suffer along with us and comfort us with His nearness if we seek Him out. It doesn't hurt to try to comfort Him once in a while, either.

With Archie not at home, my morning routine was different. Cora wouldn't let me in until fairly late in the morning as she and Mama were always up half the night. I would hang out on the front porch usually, but sometimes I would get distracted by something and have to investigate. Also, the vermin were accumulating by the back door. I had left two mice and a field rat there before I figured out that Cora wasn't going to touch them. So I changed my pattern to that of catching and eating a mouse early in the morning instead of bringing one home. This worked out well because Cora was so late in feeding me, and also because there is nothing in the world so wonderful to eat as a mouse. It is God's Perfect Food. Once I had started with that routine I wasn't eating so much of the cat food, and Cora thought my eating was off because I missed Archie. I suppose there was something to that as well. Cora got Mr. Williams who lived next door to get rid of my little corpses, the men at the fried chicken place managed to get along without Archie and me, and life more or less went on.

Archie got home about a week later looking battered, but as though he would live. Boy, was I glad to see him. He was still pale, but his abdomen was a lot smaller. He was a lot weaker, and his hands had almost stopped shaking. He had to endure quite a series of lectures from Cora about the evils of whiskey and how he had better not start that up again. Mama encouraged him to start going to church, and to put his faith and trust in the Lord. His appetite had returned, and it was only then that I realized that it had dropped off substantially over the previous year or more. He stayed home for a few days but one morning we hit the road for the coffee and fellowship. It was grand seeing him together with his pals again. Standing out in the parking lot I heard him tell one of the fellows that he had gotten food poisoning, and that he had thrown up so hard that he had torn open his stomach lining and hemorrhaged. I was rather surprised to hear this explanation, but I suppose it was true to the extent that whiskey is food. And a few days later I wasn't all that taken aback when we stopped at the whiskey store on the way home and picked up a half-pint, Archie no doubt thinking that it would be nice to have a little drink once and a while. I don't have to tell you we had some unpleasantness at home for a few days. Archie told Cora that she had gotten him so upset that he had to drink just to settle his nerves, and that if she wouldn't nag so much he wouldn't drink so much. Mama cried to Jesus, and I stayed outside as much as possible.

There was more trouble. It was hard to figure out what the problem was, but suddenly everyone was acting strangely serious. All I could determine at that time was that it had something to do with Lexie, and that Mama wasn't supposed to know. It was a bit of a puzzle. Lexie didn't seem to come around quite as often, and didn't seem quite so naturally ebullient. Cora acted differently around her as well. One day Mama asked Lexie if everything was all right to which Lexie replied that it was. Mama told her she looked tired, and that she needed to be sure that she get enough rest and eat properly. Emily seemed more subdued as well, but like most kids, she had already learned how to mask her feelings quite effectively. I could feel the instability in the lives of my human family. The fabric was frayed around the edges, and I realized that it could start to unravel. I wasn't getting the same comfort from my meditations either, so I started hanging out more with Sampson. In turn, we both would often go and visit Talks with Wolves, an old tom who lived with an Indian woman in the neighborhood, a few blocks away from where we lived. The houses were more run down in this area, and the people were more active at night. In fact, folks would be coming and going at several of them all night long, and it was hard to tell who lived there. Sampson said they were crack houses, and that people came there to buy and smoke crack. He said it had an effect something like whiskey but much stronger, and that once people got started on it they didn't stop. I remembered that Lexie's brother had been killed in a crack house and wondered if this was where it had happened. I stayed clear.

Talks with Wolves was the most spiritually advanced cat I had ever met. His meditations took him to unimaginable places. He had a serene disposition, and was generous in sharing his wisdom with us. We would get together after midnight several times per week and share stories until it was time to hunt, when we would separate. He had acquired much of the Ancient Lore that held the key to life's mysteries. His guardian, Mrs. Baker, was also very wise and gave counsel to many people who came to visit her. They would sit in a circle, smoke a pipe, and talk for hours. Talks with Wolves said she had been an alcoholic once, but this was before he was born. She had overcome her addiction by learning and practicing the spiritual customs of her ancestors, and by attending Alcoholics Anonymous. My ears stood straight up. I had not actually heard the word alcoholic used before, but I knew immediately what it meant. Finally I had a name to give to what was wrong with Archie. I was eager to learn more about this, but Talks with Wolves always had his own agenda. He would talk about what he wanted to talk about, and would deflect my questions with cryptic comments like "Listen to the drumbeat of your heart."

5

I sing because I'm happy;
I sing because I'm free;
For His Eye is on the sparrow,
And I know He watches me.

It was a cold winter by my standards. The ground froze several times, and once when we had a snowfall it stayed on the ground a week or more, instead of melting by the next day. This created some discomfort, but I still went out as usual. There were many nights I would have liked to come right back in, but it was difficult to attract the attention of my caretakers who were either inebriated, crippled, deaf, asleep, or some combination thereof. I won't say that I ever actually got used to the cold, but I learned to tolerate it and accept it as one of life's hardships. It seemed unnecessary to me that it get so cold, and I heard a lot of grumbling from other cats and people. One good thing was that I didn't have to worry about fleas in the winter.

Archie's "little drink once in a while" had turned into more like a quart of whiskey or more per day, and he was going down hill quickly. His hands would shake terribly in the morning. His routine was to stumble to the bathroom, relieve himself, rinse his mouth out with mouthwash, swallow it, gag and dry heave several times, and then vibrate back to his room and take a big drink of whiskey. Once he had figured out that he always threw up the first drink of the morning, he never wasted it with whiskey again. Cora and Mama tried their best to ignore this morning ritual, but they couldn't help but hear since their room was right next to the bathroom; and since Archie always got up early they were both still in bed. It didn't take long for him to look sick again. Once more his abdomen became distended and his color was poor. I noticed that the whites of his eyes had acquired a faintly yellow

34

tinge. He could never eat until the evening meal when he would manage to choke down a little food. Many mornings he was unable to get himself together in time to go to the fried chicken place, but we always made a run at least to the whiskey store. Cora had started to have to rely on Mrs. Williams next door to do her shopping and errands for her. It was getting obvious to me and to everyone else that this couldn't go on much longer.

One morning in early spring, I returned from my late night prowl to a heavenly chorus of mockingbirds. Life was in the air. There was a heavy dew on the ground, and I got pretty well soaked going through the high grass in my favorite mousing field down the street from our house. The crabapple trees had burst into full bloom, and the fragrance of other spring flowers hung heavily in the cool air. I ate the lovely little mouse I caught, went home, stretched out on the front porch, and treated myself to a fine washing. Eventually Archie let me in, and when he went back to bed I jumped up on my new favorite place, a little footstool that Cora had gotten for Mama and put by her chair. My glorious nap was later disturbed by the sounds of Cora and Mama stirring about. Their rising was quite a production. Neither one of them was particularly ambulatory so the least activity took forever. Cora would help Mama to her bedside commode, change her gown and give her a washing before straightening her bed linens. Sometimes Mama would want to get back in the bed, but usually she would sit in her chair and put her feet up. Then Cora would set up a TV tray and bring Mama her orange juice.

By now Cora was using a walker all the time. This turned each formerly simple task into a complicated ordeal. Take, for instance, emptying Mama's pot. Cora struggled to bend over far enough to extract the pot from under the commode, and then, holding the pot with its contents in one hand and the walker in the other, she gradually made her way to the bathroom. It was push the walker two inches forward, lean to the left and swing her right foot forward two inches, lean heavily on the walker and her right foot while she dragged her left foot forward two inches, and wave the pot around as she slowly swayed along, grunting with every movement. She barely had enough breath to mutter "Lawd have mercy" occasionally. Once in the bathroom she would empty the pot, wash it out, grunt her way back to return it to its place, and then slowly work her way back to the bathroom to wash her hands. From there she went in slow motion to the kitchen where she fixed Mama her grits and fish (an excellent breakfast in my opinion) put it on a plate, and slowly returned to the bedroom, grunting, swaying, perspiring, and wincing in pain with each step. Then it was time to get Mama her medicine, turn on the radio, fix Mama's hair, and go back to the kitchen to wash the dishes and get herself something to eat. I think she would have liked to put out my food and change my water also, but It was so hard for her to get around and bend over that caring for me was the one thing she still left for Archie She would sometimes pick things up from the floor by dragging a chair over to wherever she needed to be, sit down, lean over while holding onto the walker with one hand, and pick up the desired object. I'm sure she could have managed the dry cat food in this manner, but the water would have been more of a challenge, to say nothing of what would have been involved in emptying the litter box that I still used occasionally. After Cora had her breakfast which was usually juice and cereal, she did her dishes, and then went back to the bathroom where she did her own bathing, dressing, and fixing of her hair. Then it was time to see about Mama again, and to start lunch. Archie used to help her a lot more but his hands shook too badly in the morning, and by the time he had settled himself down with whiskey Cora didn't want to be around him.

After my nap that morning I went to check on Archie who was still in his bed, trembling madly. I jumped up and rubbed against him a couple of times, which he barely acknowledged. He was perspiring profusely. The bottle sat empty on the floor next to his bed, and he was mumbling something to himself. As I lay down at the foot of his bed he started to holler for Cora. After a few minutes in which they hollered back and forth she finally gave in and I could hear her slowly making her way to his room. She took one look inside and said she was going to call the ambulance to carry him to the hospital. He told her not to and they had a nice little disagreement about that until Cora asked him if he wanted her to just wait until he died and then she would call the undertaker. Archie was silent for a few moments. He turned in the bed and half-propped himself up on an elbow, looking at her imploringly. He had reached the point of complete defeat, and as this feeling penetrated into the very marrow of his bones he looked her in the eye and said quietly, "Cora, I need you to call AA for me."

She stared at him for a long time, their eyes meeting each other intently, profoundly engaged in the depth of despair in their lives. Finally, Cora turned without a word, and slowly made her way to the telephone. Archie forced himself out of the bed to wash and get dressed. Cora told him that someone would be over later that afternoon. Archie didn't even try to go out and get a drink that day, but he was very restless. He paced back and forth, drank a lot of juice, tried to watch TV, went to the bathroom several times, and lay down in bed from time to time. His hands continued to shake, violently at times, and he constantly wiped the perspiration from his face and neck. I was restless myself and had one of those days where when I was in I wanted to be out, and when I was out I wanted to be in.

Late in the afternoon while Archie and I were on the front porch, a car stopped in front of the house. A nicely dressed man got out, came up the steps, and walked over to Archie. He was smiling as he extended his hand.

"Are you Archie?" he asked. He grasped Archie's hand firmly.

Archie looked at him with a puzzled expression on his face and didn't answer.

"My name is Jim, and I'm an alcoholic. I'm with AA, and I'd like to help you if you want help," he said.

Archie continued to look up at him in bewilderment, still holding onto his hand. Finally he spoke. "What's a white man like you doing trying to help a nigger like me?" he said.

"The color of a man's skin is not important," Jim calmly replied. "What is important is that when someone calls out for help, that the hand of AA be there. All of us in AA are responsible to help others, and this work helps us to stay sober."

Archie regarded him for a long time without saying anything, his hand still in Jim's grasp. Finally, he got up and invited Jim into the house. Naturally, I went along as well. We sat in the living room, and they talked for a very long time. Jim started out by telling Archie all about his own life, and how he had become an alcoholic. He shared many examples of the ways in which alcohol had made his life unmanageable, and his many failed attempts to control his own drinking. Archie listened attentively. I later heard Archie say that Jim was the first person he had ever talked to who understood what his life was like. He nodded frequently as he listened to Jim's story. Jim talked about arguing with his wife, of going on terrific sprees while traveling for his job, of checking the newspaper first thing in the morning to find out not only what day it was, but what city he was in, of trips to the hospital, and of his kids hating him. Finally, his wife had him arrested after he had gotten out his gun and alternatively threatened to shoot himself, shoot her, or shoot both of them. As he sat in jail his boss had appeared and had brought with him a man from AA. This man had told Jim his own story of devastation due to drinking, and that he had found a new way of life. He told him that God had done for him what he could not do for himself. Jim had tried to write him off as a religious fanatic, but the man insisted that he didn't have to be of any particular religion. All that was required was that he be willing to believe in a power greater than himself. That didn't seem too hard to swallow, and he had been able to have an open mind about that point. His boss had told Jim that he could keep his job only if he stayed sober. He didn't tell Jim that he had to go to AA, but he strongly suggested it, and Jim decided that he would give it a try as nothing else he had tried on his own had worked for very long.

That had all happened several years ago, Jim told Archie. He had started attending AA meetings, had met many fine people, and he so far had never felt the need to take another drink. He returned to work and gradually gained the trust and confidence of his boss. He had since received several promotions. The home life improved more slowly as his family was very hurt and angry after many years of his destructive drinking, but he now was very close with most of his relations. He still had one son who showed a lot of resentment towards him, but that particular son now has the same disease that Jim has. Jim told Archie that he is still an alcoholic, and will remain so until the day he dies. But he also said he knows that he will not drink as long as he follows the spiritual principles of the AA program. At length, Jim asked Archie if he wanted to try his way of life, and Archie asked what he would have to do. Jim suggested that they pray together, and they both got down on their knees right there in the living room. As they held hands, Jim asked God to show them His Love and Mercy, and to help Archie to stop drinking. It was a brief prayer. I think he said a few more things, but very shortly he helped Archie back into his seat. As the tears were flowing down Archie's face Jim left him for a few minutes, and went to the back of the house to speak with Cora and Mama. When he returned, he told Archie that he was going to take him to the hospital. He was afraid that in his weakened physical condition he might go into DTs unless he got the right kind of medical attention. Archie got up without argument, packed a little bag, and they left together.

Archie was gone a lot longer this time. Cora didn't go to visit him at all at the hospital. She told everyone that she couldn't leave Mama alone. Everyone knew this wasn't true, as Lexie or at least a half-dozen other people would have been happy to keep Mama company for a couple of hours. I think it was her self-consciousness that kept her away, for the most part. A counselor called her a couple of times too, but Cora gave her the brush-off. The last thing she would ever get involved in was discussing her personal life with a stranger. She did fret quite a lot about Archie, and he called every few days to talk to her on the phone. I was strangely calm throughout this period. My meditations were deep and comforting, and I felt hopeful. Mrs. Williams came over every morning to help Cora with a few things including my food, water, and litter box. Lexie came over almost every day to visit and help out. Usually she either fixed dinner or brought something she had already made. Cora would sometimes fuss about what she brought and say Mama couldn't eat it for some reason or other. Lexie would bring news about Archie. She or Lenny seemed to go see him regularly, and always the report was positive. Lexie and Mama encouraged Cora to get involved in Archie's treatment, but that conversation never went anywhere.

The dogwoods had bloomed and faded and the critters were already well into raising their first nestlings before Archie came home. It was uncomfortable at first for everyone, as a new routine had been established that he had to break into. I was glad to see Archie looking so healthy, and I should have given him a big welcome, but since I am a cat and not a dog, I ignored him for a day or two. Quickly, though, things were much as they were before, or at least, as they had been about a year before. We were making our morning run to the fried chicken place, running errands, visiting Lexie, and taking our requisite naps. Archie was helping Cora around the house again, and going on the afternoon run. One difference was that Archie went out every evening. Sometimes Jim would come by for him, and other times he would go on his own. Often he would come home smelling strongly of cigarette smoke, which was strange because Archie didn't smoke. He had some new books that he read every day, something to do with AA, I guess, because he and Jim would study one of them together fairly often.

At first, when Jim came over to visit they always sat in the living room, but after a while they started sitting out on the front porch. I think Archie was self-conscious about having a white man come over to his house on a social basis, and it took him a while to get over it. This is odd because Lenny was a frequent visitor, but I suppose the difference is that Lenny was family. Cora's main advice to Archie was that he should spend less time reading those AA books and more time reading the Bible, a book I never saw her pick up in all the years I lived with her. Her corollary advice was that he didn't need all those AA meetings, but did need to start going to church. I never heard her tell him she was glad he had quit drinking, and when Jim or his other AA friends came over she stayed in the back of the house. For a good long while we all lived a little bit on the edge, waiting for him to start drinking again, but eventually, Archie's abstemiousness came to seem as natural as his habitual inebriation had seemed previously. Mama would praise God for it from time to time and tell Archie he was doing fine and to stick with AA. Cora was such a negative person that even though I know she was grateful, I never heard her utter one word of support to Archie for what he was doing. As I have said before, she was the sort that couldn't tolerate well-being, and if things stayed good too long, she would stir up some kind of mess or other.

I'm sure you know what a reflex action is. It's when A is always automatically followed by B. My favorite example is Mama always saying "Oh, Lawd" immediately after I start yakking. Cats frequently like to clear their stomachs, sometimes to expel a fur ball, but usually just on general principles. So every once in a while I would start to retch, and the very next thing I would hear was "Oh, Lawd." I had my favorite places for this purgative activity, but the best was the oriental carpet in the living room. Once when I was fairly young I had started while on Cora's bed (where I was always unwelcome anyway), and came closer to a premature demise than at any time in my life. I learned that lesson well. Mama always heard me first mainly because she was the only one of the three of them who could hear well enough to speak of. If she could attract someone's attention soon enough an effort would be made to shoo me out of the house before my yakking was productive. This was very irritating to me, as there are certain times when I just don't like to be interrupted. I guess it is just one of those unpleasant interfaces between cats and people. Once I cleared my stomach, a cleaning activity would immediately ensue, complete with grumbling, scolding, grunting, and spraying of chemicals. Archie was the designated stomach contents remover, and to his credit, the only thing he ever grumbled about was the others getting so upset about the whole thing. His philosophy was that cats throw up, people clean it up, and life goes on. He couldn't see any more sense to getting upset about it than anything else that occurs in the natural order of things. He was certainly right except that for some people getting upset over the natural order of things is the natural order of things. I must admit I have known a few cats like this as well.

As time went on in my life, I had more frequent visions in meditation of the woman who looked like Lexie. One of the most disturbing was in a field where dozens of black people were setting out plants. A white man rode about on a horse, yelling, threatening, and cursing. It was hot and no one was allowed to rest even for a moment; and no water was available to drink as the sweat poured off of their bodies. Suddenly the man began to yell at the Lexie-lady, and her hands began to tremble. She must have made some kind of mistake, and after he started yelling at her she was so upset that she did something else wrong. The next thing I knew, he was hitting her with a horsewhip (which should never be used on a horse either). He must have hit her thirty times or more, in an uncontrollable rage. He could easily have killed her. The most chilling aspect of the whole experience was watching the other slaves go on working as though nothing was happening out of the ordinary. Their facial expressions told the whole story. One man in particular who stood nearby must have been her husband. He seemed to be consumed with shame and fury, helpless to protect her. That night in another meditation I saw her back and shoulders terribly swollen, covered with deep red marks. Some other women were smearing some kind of grease on her and trying to get her to eat something. A woman said that God would hear their prayers and deliver them, just as He had the children of Israel. But the lady of my vision was in shock. I could feel from her the conviction that she was doomed to die a slave, to never know freedom in this world. She recovered somewhat from that beating, but as I continued to see her she looked weak and pale, and did die the following winter, still a young woman. I tell you, these were troubling visions, and I got little comfort sharing them with my mentors, Sampson and Talks With Wolves. Sometimes I can be philosophical about the coexistence of kindness and cruelty, good and evil, life and death, and sometimes my little cat heart wants to explode.

6

Tell me didn't it rain, children;
Rain, oh my Lord, didn't it.

We were in one of those life-cycles of calmness and serenity seemingly caused by nothing more than the relative absence of anything going particularly wrong. Archie especially was a changed person. He had an incredible amount of energy, and actually spent a lot less time at home than previous to his recovery. I still went with him on his morning rounds, and we still stopped by to visit Lexie fairly often. I started to get curious about where he went after dinner, so one night I followed him out of the house and jumped into the car. We drove to a little church not far from home. Archie told me I had to stay outside which I did, but not for long. The people inside seemed quite cheerful. They all seemed to know Archie. They sat around for a long time talking and drinking coffee, and seemed to think I was pretty cute. I did some exploring inside the church, and decided it would be a fine place to do some serious mousing if I ever got the opportunity. That expedition went so well, from Archie's point of view, that he often took me with him thereafter. I got to know a lot of his friends, and saw Jim from time to time. Once in a while Mrs. Baker was at one of the places we went. At that place they always burned sage before they started their meeting. It seemed to have a positive effect on the spiritual energy in the room. Over a period of time I saw many people come and go, unable to integrate the music of their own souls with that of the fellowship. I think more stayed than left, overall, and my observation is that those people who connected with the community of recovering people were the ones who opened themselves up to hearing God, as opposed to criticizing or ignoring Him. Of course, none of them had a clue about the cat being the true child of God, but there are degrees of enlightenment, and that is as it should be.

Grits had a new litter and I hadn't seen her for a few days, so I dropped by at Mrs. Johnson's house and scratched at the door until she let me in. At first Grits hissed at me, out of her natural instincts, but we were so close that she was able to tolerate me being around her kittens. They were all adorable, and for that matter, so was she, the way she fussed over them. The cutest one was a little black and white number who must have been mine. She was the smallest one, but also the most curious and talkative. As she feverishly glanced around and explored, her whole being seemed to say "What's that, what's that, what's that?" Everything held her utmost fascination for about three-quarters of a second. Grits was forever retrieving her from her little forays, washing her, and scolding her. It reminded me of my own kittenhood many years earlier. Mrs. Johnson gave me a treat, but I didn't stay too long, as Grits wasn't much in the mood for adult company. I decided to check in on her again in a few days.

It was late summer, what people refer to as the dog days. That means it was insufferably hot and nasty. Everyone was irritable, even the mice. One night Sampson and I went over to where Talks with Wolves lived. There was more than the usual amount of traffic in and out of the crack houses, so it must have been a Saturday night. We were lying in the grass feeling the atmosphere suffused with the raw excitement and irritability of the crack addicts, and the contrasting lethargy caused by the excessive heat. Suddenly Talks with Wolves laid his ears back. I felt it too, a sense of alarm, a feeling that something was about to happen. I could feel myself bristle. Within seconds there was a muffled pop-pop-popping sound that came from inside the house directly behind where we were communing. Within seconds, several people came rushing out. Some of them got into cars and drove quickly off, but most of them ran. Not long after a siren wailed, heralding the arrival of the police. Several squad cars arrived, and soon after, an ambulance, like the one that comes for Mama. We didn't hang around, as the energy in the atmosphere was too disagreeable to tolerate for very long.

I was in a state of radical amazement such as I had never been in my life, either before or since. My shock was not because of the shooting, because that sort of thing happened over there from time to time. No, I was stunned because the very first person who tore out of the crack house after the shooting was none other than Lenny Solomon. He didn't get very far either. By the time he got to the end of the rather long block the cops were there, and he was stopped. We saw the whole thing. He had to get out of the car, lie on the ground, and go through all the rigmarole that the cops put everyone through in that neighborhood when they stop them. They even put his hands behind his back and handcuffed him. One of the cops went through Lenny's car, and he was put in the squad car. I waited as long as I could possibly tolerate to see what would happen, but eventually had to go on. None of us cats said anything to each other, but we were all thinking the same thing..."Boy, is Lexie going to be pissed!" But beyond that I felt very sad. I liked Lenny and loved his family. They were in for a lot of heartache. It wasn't just the embarrassment of getting arrested. I had hung around the crack houses for a long time, and I had seen the crack addicts come to the AA meetings, so I knew what they were all in for. Many of them didn't quit until they had lost everything, and most of the ones I saw never quit at all. There would be periods of time where they would, either because they were in jail, or were trying hard to go straight. But sooner or later they would be back smoking that crack again, getting sicker and sicker, thinner and thinner, and spiritually more and more bankrupt. A few did seem to succeed in getting their lives on track and keeping them that way, but just because Lenny was basically a nice guy with a good family, there was no guarantee of success.

Before dawn I went through the motions of catching a mouse and brought it home for Archie. We made our morning trip to the fried chicken place for coffee and fellowship, and went home. I apprehensively waited for the proverbial stuff to hit the fan. It was Sunday morning, and for some time now Mama had been too decrepit to go to church, but still it was a special day for her. The radio was blasting out sermons and songs of praise. She still got a lot of company on Sunday, so Cora fussed over her in slow motion most of the morning to get her presentable. Around nine-thirty the phone rang. Mama answered it as usual, because first of all she was the only one who normally heard it ring, and second of all because most of the calls were for her. Up until that summer when Archie got involved in AA, all the calls were for her. So Mama called Archie to pick up the phone and said it was Lenny. After Mama hung up I jumped off her bed and ran into Archie's room. He mostly listened with a serious expression on his face, and then told Lenny he would be there as soon as he could, and that he would bring Lexie. Evidently, Lenny tried to talk him out of that but Archie was insistent and told him he was just going to have to deal with it. He hung up and called Lexie who, of course, was frantic because Lenny hadn't come home the previous night. Archie told her Lenny had called from jail, he didn't know what charge, and he would be over to pick her up in a few minutes. We went to the kitchen where Cora was finishing the breakfast dishes, and he told her what he knew of what had happened. Her eyes stretched and she said, "Lawd, this gonna kill Mama. I guess I better tell her befo' the phone ring and she hear it from someone else. Bad news sho' do travel fast." Archie wouldn't let me come with him so I went back to the house and scratched at the door, it seemed forever, until Cora let me back in. She was in a foul mood and scolded me. Mama was crying when I got back to her room. The phone rang constantly, but Cora wouldn't let anyone talk to Mama, and was less and less diplomatic about it as the day wore on.

There was also a parade of busybodies coming through the front door. With Archie gone, Cora had to answer the door, and was exhausted by mid-afternoon. Mrs. Williams from next door took over the duties of hostess to the curious mob.

So I had another one of those days where I was depressed and worried, where when I was in I wanted out, and when I was out I wanted in. Mostly I was out since Archie wasn't home and Cora ignored me when I scratched at the door. I guess she thought she had enough on her hands with Mama crying and the telephone ringing constantly. I managed to piece together over the next few days what had happened that day. Archie had gone over to meet Lexie, who had also called Lenny's parents, Cecilia and Abe Solomon. Archie had also called his sponsor, Jim, who in turn had called the hospital where he had taken Archie. Jim had done some excellent work coaching the family, as well as giving them some comfort and hope. They went down to the jail and discovered that Lenny was not being held on the shooting charge, just some drug charges, and it was an easy matter to bail him out. However, Lenny had to agree to go directly to the hospital, or either stay in jail. He made some feeble objections about work, but they didn't hold water since he worked for Abe who wasn't about to be snowed by that line. Also, he knew he was in too much hot water, and he figured he'd probably be better off in the hospital than having to go home and deal with Lexie just then. At Jim and Archie's suggestion they requested Doctor Wilson who was an older physician and himself a recovering alcoholic. It had been a tough day for the family, but people usually discover that when troubles come, all they can do is face up to them as best as they can, and most people do pretty well.

For the next several weeks, Archie spent a lot of time with Lexie, talking to her and telling her what he had learned in the process of his own early recovery from alcoholism. I often went with him, and noticed that she wasn't looking too good. For that matter, I don't think she had looked that great for a while. She seemed to be tired all the time, and was getting those dark circles under her eyes. She didn't have the same sparkle in her personality. On one of our visits over there I was up in her room nosing around when she came upstairs to change clothes, and I noticed that on her chest there was a long scar where a part had been removed. It was the same sort of thing as with Grits and her tail, except that I was a little taken aback when I saw Lexie like that because when she was wearing her clothes you couldn't tell anything was missing. So I had no idea that had happened to her. She had a thing she kept in a box that she put in her clothing so you couldn't tell the part was missing. It was the breast, the part that human females provide milk to their babies with. People have only two because they don't have big litters like cats do. Lexie looked at herself in the mirror for a moment before she dressed. I wouldn't exactly say she made a face, but she did look very sad, and I felt badly for her. She was such a lovely person. Sometimes I wish life didn't have to be so difficult, but of course, God couldn't provide joy without agony as its opposite. I discovered that Lexie was going to her own doctor every few weeks for what they called "chemo." Usually Archie would take her, but once in a while Cecilia did. I gather that chemo is some kind of strong medicine because you could depend on Lexie being sick for a couple of days afterwards.

Archie and I often picked Lexie up to take her to visit Lenny at the hospital. It was a pretty nice place. There were several buildings on a well-landscaped campus. They had some dumb rule about pets not being allowed inside, but the people were friendly and liked to give me treats. Some of them had strange ideas about what I might like to eat, and at times I had to politely refuse. There were a few other cats that seemed to hang around there, and they were none too friendly to me. They thought they owned the place. But I had as much right to be there as any other cat, and I didn't mind telling them so.

Sometimes Emily came along. She always griped about having to go. I felt sorry for her. She was getting lost in the shuffle, with so much going on in the lives of her parents. I know that kids need to learn to deal with hardship as they are developing, or they never will be able to cope with life as adults, just as it is for cats. Parents want to protect them as much as possible, and when not possible, teach them to cope, with God's help. But her parents were both struggling with their own stuff just then. I think she got most of her support from her own friends. Emily had two other major stresses in her life at that time. One was just being twelve years old, with everything that involves. The other was getting ready for her Bat Mitzvah. I heard them talk about it, but didn't really get what it was all about until it happened several months later. Twice a week Lexie picked her up after school and took her to Hebrew school where she studied about Lenny's religion. She was also learning to read the Hebrew Bible for her Bat Mitzvah ceremony. When Lexie was too sick, Cecilia or Archie would pick her up and take her. This appeared to be a rather joyless pursuit for Emily, or tedious at best. But as in most things, there seemed to be a good side to it. I began to hear them talking about having a big party and inviting all her friends and relatives. She also had the expectation of getting many wonderful presents. So despite her feeling lost and ignored in her current family circumstances, she did have a time to look forward to where she would be center-stage.

One day I was curled up at the foot of Mama's bed listening to the Morning Sounds of Praise, when Brother Parker played a song we hadn't heard before, "Hey y'all, how y' bin doin', since y' bin filled with the Holy Ghost?" Cora and Mama both seemed amused. Cora said, "Mama, do you 'member ol' Po' Boy Smith who lived out in the country past the mountain? He used to always say 'Hey, y'all'."

Mama chuckled. "Yes, Lawd, we used to go out there and buy chickens fo' ten cents apiece. He'd even wring their necks so's we wouldn't have to. He always said 'Hey, y'all,' and had a big smile for everyone."

"Can't buy no chicken fo' no ten cents no mo'," said Cora.

"No Lawd," Mama replied, shaking her head slowly back and forth. She paused for a moment as though deep in thought. "But folks still sayin' 'Hey y'all'."

They both laughed. (Now that I think of it, laughter is one of the gifts God gave to people that he didn't share with cats. I wonder why.) After a while Mama spoke again, looking concerned.

"Cora," she said, "I'm worried about Lexie. She just don't look right. Seems like she's tired all the time. What do you s'pose is wrong with her? I hope she's not sick."

"I know what you talkin' about Mama," replied Cora, taking a deep breath. She knew Mama couldn't fail to notice how poorly Lexie was looking, and dreaded what would happen if she found out the truth.

Secretly she hoped God had enough sense to make sure Mama died first, and after thinking this she would feel horribly guilty and fear that God would punish her. But Cora had an obvious card to play. "Well, Mama, I s'pose she just stays worried about Lenny and all that mess he got himself into. But she sho do look wo' out."

"Yes, Lawd," said Mama, "Mm, mm, mm!" She shook her head again and started to cry. "I just pray for that child all the time, asking God to take care of her and the baby."

I got up and rubbed against her, purring. Mama was so old and had had such a hard life. You would like to think that it could get easier, and I think it does at times. But once people (and cats) get really old, it seems to get harder again. And it isn't just the physical infirmities. I had heard Cora say that if Mama found out about Lexie it would kill her, and she meant it literally. I'm not sure how convinced Mama was that there was nothing else wrong with Lexie, but she didn't pursue it, and Cora distracted her by asking her what she wanted for lunch.

Lenny was in the hospital for a long time, but he did get to come home once in a while, and once he came over to our place for Sunday dinner. He was in good spirits, and didn't seem to mind when Mama asked him how things were going with his treatment. The only person who seemed uncomfortable with the subject was Cora, who scowled at whomever brought it up. It turned out that after a few weeks, Lenny got sent to another place where he lived with some other guys he had been in treatment with, and he lived there for a very long time, almost until Emily's Bat Mitzvah.

7

The river Jordan is deep and wide,
Hallelujah!
Milk and honey on the other side,
Hallelujah!

Every so often, Talks with Wolves would invite a few of us together for a Summer Gathering. It consisted of some prayers, silent meditation, and a story from the Ancient Lore. The Gathering was always on a cloudless night, and heralded by the insistent call of a chuck-will's widow. Talks with Wolves would prepare himself for the event with a day of fasting and prayer, and we were all expected to do the same. At the sound of our herald, we all would gather in a field down the street from his house, and draw around our storyteller for our lesson. Talks with Wolves would bring the feather of a mockingbird with him. He would start by brushing each of us with it, and he held it in his fore paws as he spoke. Our field contained many wild flowers and herbs that fostered positive energy for our gathering. One night around the time all this was going on we had such a Summer Gathering. I had had a fairly normal day for those times, but I wasn't myself. The feeling of depression and fear of impending doom lay deeply within me as my people struggled so with their lives. The previous evening Talks with Wolves had let several of us know that he was holding a Summer Gathering the following night. He could always tell the signs when it was time again. I didn't give it too much thought, but did leave the house without touching my dry cat food, taking in nothing but water all day. The hunger didn't bother me too much, probably because of my depression, but I did have a hard time getting myself in the proper meditative state preparatory for the event.

These sessions always dealt with ancient stories, often about the times not long after the Creation when God was ordering the world. He would tell us about the heroic deeds and adventures of First Cat, our primal ancestor. I stayed away from the house most of the day so as to clear my mind, and to avoid the fussing which I would have to endure about not eating. I visited Grits and discovered that she had been invited for the first time, and was planning to attend. It was a hot and muggy day with no breeze. We were well into summer then, and most of the animals had already raised their young, so were less purposeful in their activities. It was so hot that day that the dogs didn't even want to expend enough energy to bark. I moved from one shady place to the next until it was dark. I thought about swinging by home just to check up on everything but didn't because there was the chance that I wouldn't be able to get back out in time. Anyway, I needed to be clearing my mind of daily worries, not adding them in. The locusts and other insects were making quite a racket that night, and as always on such a night, about two hours after dark, the owls set up a low, rhythmic hooting. This always helped me get into the proper mood, and I found a big hydrangea shrub to lie under where I floated between napping and meditating for a couple of hours. The call of the chuck-will's widow stirred me. I stopped by to pick up Grits and we proceeded to the field. Sampson was already there along with a few other cats I knew from the neighborhood. The last to arrive was Talks with Wolves. He led a brief prayer in which he thanked God for the evening, for ordering the world as He had, and asked Him to let His Spirit be with us that evening. He thanked Him for His wondrous creation, the mouse, and he thanked the mouse for its participation in the grand design of life. We each in turn rubbed our chins and flanks in catnip leaves that Talks with Wolves had brought, in order to cancel any negative energy that we might have brought into the circle. Then Talks with Wolves purified the mockingbird feather with the catnip, brushed each of us with it, lay down, placed it under his fore paws, and closed his eyes.

"Many, many years ago," he began, "the world was a primeval place, new, with no ancient history. God had just formed it, causing physical matter to appear from the energy of His own Spirit. There was sky, which consisted of sun, moon, stars, and the vast expanse. And there was earth, which consisted of water, land, and fire. At the interface between these two worlds was rain, wind, and light. God made and blessed them all, and placed living things in the world. He planted a garden of grasses, trees, flowers, ferns, and shrubs. He made the flying creatures, and those which creep on the ground; and He populated the oceans, lakes, and streams with fishes and other water-breathing sorts of things. God was pleased with what He had done as He surveyed His new world, and sent His Holy Spirit out to the animals, plants, and rocks, making Himself known to them. The world was as it should be, as God had designed it, consistent with His purposes, according to His divine plan."

Talks with Wolves paused and looked around at us, and satisfied that he had everyone's complete attention, he continued.

"First Cat was happy in his new home. He had discovered it contained many wondrous things to explore and enjoy, delicious little creatures to chase and eat, lovely sounds and scents to absorb. There were females to mate with. None of the other males were as strong or fast as he was, so he always had the best of the females and fathered the best kittens. Life was entirely pleasurable, filled with all the joys of the world, and with the presence of God. Then one day as First Cat was lying in a grassy field on a sunny day, a hawk appeared to him and spoke.

" 'First Cat,' said Hawk, 'a great evil is threatening our new and wonderful world. Soon a blight will fall upon all the plants, causing them to wither and die. Then the plant-eating creatures will sicken from eating the diseased plants, and the flesh-eating creatures will sicken as well. Devastation and death will reign everywhere as the Holy Spirit of God will be forced to leave His creation. He has sent me to you as the only one left who can save our world. In a far off land there is a crystal with great healing power. If you can travel to this land, get the crystal, and bring it back here to a place I will show you, the energy from the crystal will drive out the evil that threatens us. But there is great danger in this journey. You will have to cross a great and powerful river, climb steep, icy mountains, and travel through a forest filled with dangerous dogs and bears.'

"Hawk led First Cat to the top of a hill covered with hemlock and cedar, except that the very top of the hill was free of trees. Instead, it consisted of a flat rock several meters square. There were two perpendicular lines intersecting exactly at the center, and at that spot was a depression or groove.

" 'The crystal must be placed at the center of this rock,' said Hawk. 'You have exactly three months to complete your journey and return to this place. The crystal must be in its place on high noon of the day of the summer solstice. If you succeed, when the sun strikes the crystal at precisely the right angle on that day, the energy released will drive away the blight, and all will be right in the world again. If you fail, we all shall perish.'

"First Cat walked on the rock and sniffed at the groove. He could detect nothing unusual about its scent to indicate its power. He glanced back at Hawk. 'Why am I being sent?' he asked.

" 'Many have already tried and failed. Raccoon, Dog, Bear, and Man have each been defeated by the rigors of the journey, in one way or another. The last hope is that you will succeed where the others have failed. If you do succeed, then you will find special favor in God's sight. You and all your succeeding generations will occupy a favored place in the world.'

"First Cat was filled with doubt and fear. How could he succeed where the others had failed? What if the world did wither and die, and it was his fault? The responsibility was too great. Hawk read his thoughts.

" 'Yes, it is a great responsibility,' he said. 'You are being called upon to be responsible for your own life as well as the lives of others. You will succeed if you face your fears. Besides, you will not go alone. Wait here,' he said.

"Hawk turned and flew off to the north. He was gone rather a long time, causing First Cat to wonder if he had imagined the whole thing. At length, Hawk returned, flying from the east. He had a small amount of white rabbit fur in his beak. In the talons of his right foot he carried some grass, and in the left he had sage. He placed these articles on the rock, and he reached down to pull three small feathers from his chest. Taking the grass, he quickly wove a pouch for the fur, and then tied the pouch, sage, and feathers together in a small bundle. With the last of the grass, he tied the bundle around the neck of First Cat.

" 'As long as you carry these charms you will be safe,' said Hawk. 'And you will meet many in your travels who will help you. But beware, for there will also be those who will try to deceive you.'

" 'How will I know the way?' inquired First Cat. He still wasn't too sure he wanted to take on this challenge.

" 'You will be led,' replied Hawk, stretching his wings out wide. 'I will get you started in the right direction. When I have to let you go on, there will be others to guide you. At times it will seem that you are lost. At those times you must follow your own heart and be brave.'

" 'How will I know where to look for the crystal?' asked First Cat.

" 'After you cross the river, the mountains, and the forest,' said Hawk, 'you will come to a castle overlooking a beautiful meadow. The crystal is kept within the highest tower of the castle. But beware, for the castle is controlled by a powerful and dangerous evil spirit in the form of a witch, and guarded by many fierce creatures with strong magic. Man was the only one who even got as far as the castle, but he failed to penetrate its defenses and returned empty-handed.'

"First Cat sighed. He thought about his idyllic life where everything had been provided for him in abundance, where every moment was pleasurable. He had never thought that life would be any different, never considered that he would struggle or want for anything. He never thought about responsibility. He was afraid, and with every ounce of his being he wished that he could be excused from this task, and return to the easy life. He looked at Hawk, and Hawk looked back at him with a firm, unrelenting gaze. There was no place to hide. He said a quick prayer asking God to be with him on his journey, to give him strength and wisdom when he needed it, and to comfort him where he was afraid. 'Thy Will be done' concluded his prayer.

" 'All right,' he said, 'I'm ready.'

"Before dawn the next morning First Cat stirred. He caught and ate a mouse, and at the first graying of the morning, he set off. He started along a stream bank, but as it meandered too much, he left it to cross a field in a westerly direction, as Hawk had told him to follow the sun. Looking up, he spotted Hawk soaring high overhead towards the west, but it wasn't long before he circled back, dipped his wings in acknowledgment of First Cat, and flew off to the east. All day long First Cat pushed forward, stopping occasionally for water or rest. Despite his anxiety, he did have a sense of excitement at such an adventure. Whenever he thought about the danger, he remembered that he had the magical charms given him by Hawk, and also that God was with him. He did wonder whether the others had any magic with them, and certainly God must have been with them too. He could think of no answer to this mystery, and so had no choice but to proceed on faith and hope. He spent the first night in a cave, having to abandon the hollow log he had first selected to a huge raccoon. Food was plentiful along the way, and for the first two days the weather was pleasant. The second night, however, it started to rain, and a cold front blew in. First Cat had never experienced such conditions, as he had been living in Paradise where it was perfectly lovely at all times. There were no caves in the vicinity, so he crawled under some dense underbrush where he was fairly well sheltered for the rest of the night.

"The rain continued steadily into the morning, and a harsh wind blew. First Cat wanted to stay in the underbrush, but he had a mission that couldn't wait, so he ventured out across the low hills, through the fields, crossing briskly flowing clear streams. Water clung to everything, and First Cat was soaked through to his skin in short order. He had never been so cold or wet. He was miserable and prayed to God that the rain would stop so he could dry out and get warm again. There was no dry place to rest, and it was harder to hunt under those conditions. Had he known that the cold rain was to persist for another week without let-up, he would have despaired. Every day he had to continue through cold, wet meadows and copses, and every night he tried to rest in a wet spot out of the wind, at least. And he grew tired. First Cat had never traveled before, always living a life of ease, where everything he needed was close at hand. The tiny streams he had been crossing swelled into rushing torrents of water, which were dangerous to cross. More than once he had to crawl across logs or jump from branch to branch of fallen trees in order to continue on his journey. At night he heard wolves and the screams of mountain lions. He was forced to climb a tree to escape a pack of wild dogs late one afternoon, and had to spend the night up there, until he was certain they had given up on him and gone. Finally the rain stopped, but by now the land was flooded, and First Cat's progress had become extremely tedious. Once the sun came out he found a place on a rock to stretch out, and by the end of the day he was warm and nearly dry. He decided to rest for a couple of days to get his strength back, and at the same time let the land dry out and become more passable. The hunting there was good, and before long he was ready to set off once more. He felt extreme gratitude for the renewed pleasantness of the weather, and gave many thanks to God. He had gone through the most taxing ordeal of his life, and it occurred to him that this would probably be nothing compared to the rigors that Hawk had foretold. He tried not to think about this, but just pushed forward. He made a strenuous effort to keep his thoughts focused on his mission of finding the crystal and bringing it to the required place by high noon of the summer solstice.

"As the days wore on First Cat noticed that the terrain grew more rugged. There were rocky outcroppings, higher hills, and more dense underbrush.

He began to encounter coyotes and carefully avoided them. One day around mid-morning First Cat climbed a fairly steep hill and was overjoyed to see the first objective of his journey. There below him was a bigger river than he had ever imagined. It stretched from the north to the south as far as he could see, and it seemed to be a day's journey in width. His joy at reaching his first objective was immediately followed by bewilderment about how he could possibly get across. He stared for a long time, and thought. While no solution came to him, he did proceed down to the river's edge. The current was much faster than First Cat had expected, probably due to all the rain, and the river was well over its bank. From where he was standing he couldn't see the opposite shore. He had no idea what he was to do. He nearly despaired as he thought that he must fail in his mission at such an early stage, when everything depended on his success. As he paced back and forth sniffing at the river and the bank, wondering what to do, he encountered an otter.

" 'Who are you?' Otter inquired. He had never seen a cat before.

" 'My name is First Cat,' was the reply.

" They sniffed noses and felt safe with each other. Otter was curious.

" 'Where do you come from, and why are you here?' he wanted to know.

" 'I have traveled a long way from my home in Paradise,' he replied. 'I am on an important mission, and I have to cross the river.'

"Otter laughed. (He is one of the few creatures who can.) 'How do you expect to cross the river? It is too wide, and the current is too strong. God has made me the strongest swimmer of all the land creatures, and it would be impossible for me to cross it.'

"First Cat considered what he said. As he thought, it was impossible to swim across the river. As he looked around he noticed a large tree growing a short distance out into the water. On the one hand, he didn't see what good it would do to reach it, but on the other hand, it was closer to the other side than he was now. Otter watched him and could see what First Cat was considering.

" 'I wouldn't try that if I were you,' he said. 'I don't think you can reach it, and if you do you will be stranded until the water recedes. It won't help you get to the other side.'

"First Cat didn't doubt that he was right, but hadn't thought of anything better to try. Cautiously, he put a paw into the water, and then a second paw. The force of the current knocked him off balance, and suddenly he was swimming for his life. The pouch tied to his neck seemed to give him some buoyancy, but he quickly could tell he was fighting a losing battle. Not only could he not swim out to the tree, but neither could he swim back to the shore. As he struggled to keep his head out of the water he was saved by Otter, who had jumped into the river, grasped First Cat by the side of the neck, and towed him back to the shore.

" 'You can barely swim at all!' exclaimed Otter contemptuously.

"First cat shook himself and looked around. They were a short distance downstream from where they had started, and now he could see more trees and shrubs growing up out of the water. Once again he ventured into the water, and once again would have drowned had Otter not saved him.

" 'You are a strange animal, First Cat,' said Otter, 'and none too intelligent. Why do you try to swim if you don't know how?'

"First Cat actually could swim a little, but made no effort to explain. 'Could you help me get out to that dead tree out there?' he asked. A large fallen dead tree could be seen above the flooded river about one hundred feet from the bank.

"Otter stared at him. 'You don't get it, do you?' he said in as exasperated a tone as he could muster. 'The river can't be crossed, and you're worse off out on that tree than you are here on shore. Why don't you just forget about it?'

"First Cat took a deep breath and plunged back into the river. He struggled to swim towards the dead tree, but in no time was once again in a battle for his life. For the third time Otter swam out to save him, but this time he towed him out to the dead tree. First Cat managed to climb out of the water onto the tree, and Otter scampered up next to him.

" ' That is the last time I'm going to save you,' said Otter emphatically. 'I don't have the time for this nonsense. If you jump off this tree back into the river, you're on your own.' Otter felt a little badly for speaking so harshly, but what else could he do? The cat seemed determined to kill himself.

" 'You're right,' replied First Cat. 'Thank you so much for helping me. God will bless you for your kindness. I will have to wait out here until I can think of what to do next.'

"Otter gave him a strange look. 'Well, good luck, Cat,' he said, as he jumped off the tree and swam back to the shore.

"First Cat looked around to survey his situation. Truly, he hadn't seemed to accomplish very much, and he still couldn't see the opposite shore. He was tired, wet, and hungry. He stretched out on the dead tree, a couple of feet above the water, and slept for a long while. When he awakened he was hungry, and his muscles ached from struggling in the water. As he looked around he saw some small fish swimming next to his dead tree. He crept along the log until he was just above the river, quickly reached into the water, flipped a fish into the air, grabbed it, and held it down with his paw while it tried to flop away from him. It made a tasty little meal, and was followed by a couple more in quick succession, until he was no longer hungry, and was able to think of something besides his stomach. It was late afternoon. As First Cat looked up and down the river he noticed quite a lot of detritus from the flood floating downstream, mostly leaves and branches. Some of the branches were quite large. As he looked upstream, a large log approached, and struck the dead tree with considerable force. For a few moments it was hung up on the dead tree, and then the trailing end swung around towards the open river. Cautiously, First Cat climbed onto the log, and just as he did, it broke free, carrying him rapidly downstream. It was quite an experience, riding on the log. First Cat scrambled back and forth on it, considering what to do. Most of the time they floated freely, but at times the log would collide with other logs, or with other trees protruding from the water. It grew dark, and First Cat realized that all he could do was grip the log tightly and hope he didn't get thrown off.

"It was a long night in which he got no sleep. By the next morning, he could see that his travels on the log had kept him close to the shore. He was hungry again, and there were no fish to be seen as they sped along. As the sun rose in the sky he began to hear a strange noise, which gradually grew louder. The log seemed to pick up speed, and more detritus was noticeable. As he looked downstream, he noticed that the river seemed to narrow, and the opposite shore was in sight. The noise grew louder as the log bumped into more and more objects. He was carried downstream to a great bend in the river where there was a powerful whirlpool. His log began to ride a circular current moving faster and faster. First Cat was caught up in a huge eddy of whirling logs and branches. Some of the logs were being sucked under the water by the powerful force of the vortex. He was knocked off balance several times and had to jump from log to log. Every hair on his body was standing straight up in terror. He could not tell how long he rode the eddy, but finally found himself at the edge of the logjam, and miraculously, very close to the opposite shore. A great collision threw him into the water where at any second he could have been crushed by the spinning logs. He was pulled under water by the force of the whirlpool. All he could do was struggle to reach the surface, and hold his breath. After what seemed like an eternity, he was thrown to the surface of the river, and snagged by a protruding branch from a fallen tree on the opposite bank. He managed to crawl onto the tree and lay there exhausted for a long time. Finally, he crawled to shore, worked his way well up the bank, and stopped to catch his breath again. It was almost dark by now. He was hungry but too tired to catch anything, and was cold and wet again. He could do nothing more than find some good cover in the underbrush where he slept like one who was dead until morning."

8

All night, all day
Angels watchin' over me my Lord.
All night, all day
Angels watchin' over me.

I had grown stiff from lying in one position, and stretched rather noisily. Talks with Wolves paused in his tale. The other cats took advantage of the brief pause to rearrange themselves after stretching also. Our storyteller looked around, satisfied himself that he had our attention, and continued.

"Against what seemed like impossible odds, First Cat had completed his first challenge successfully. When he awakened, every muscle in his body ached as never before. He was also coughing frequently, and supposed that he had inhaled a little water. 'I must have almost drowned,' he thought. He was grateful to still be alive and able to pursue his quest, and felt comforted by his morning prayer, and in knowing that he carried the magic around his neck. It was a gray day, and rather cool, so he didn't dry quickly. He rested in the underbrush until dusk, sleeping most of the time. Hunger eventually overrode his fatigue, and so he gathered his strength to begin to hunt. The terrain was difficult, and different from what he was used to, but before long his instincts led him to a small rodent which he killed and ate. He then rested most of the night, trying to gain strength from his nourishment, and before dawn hunted and ate again, and felt ready enough to proceed.

"By late afternoon the sky had cleared to a deep cerulean blue, and as First Cat reached the crest of a rise he saw in the distance a great mountain range to the West. He was in awe of what was before him, and thought how great God was to have fashioned such mighty mountains. Although the mountains rose high on the horizon, it still took him several days to reach them. On the one hand this frustrated him, as he was eager to accomplish his mission, but on the other, he was anxious about how he was to cross such a high mountain range.

"One day, as he neared his objective, he stopped to drink from a clear stream. The water was cold and refreshing. First Cat paused to view his reflection, and suddenly became alarmed. The pouch was gone! Many thoughts raced through his mind at once. How had this happened? Should he retrace his steps and look for it? How could he continue without it? When had he lost it? First Cat felt lonely and afraid. He once again felt overwhelmed by his task, and he was angry with himself for being careless and thereby jeopardizing his all-important mission. He paced back and forth, sniffing and worrying. After much thought he remembered to pray, which calmed him sufficiently to think logically. He came to the conclusion that his pouch had probably come off several days previously in the river when he had been tossed about into branches and fallen trees. God had provided for him so far, and all he could do was to proceed and hope that God would continue to provide the means for him to succeed. The fact that so many other creatures had already failed did nag at him and give him doubts about himself, but he saw no alternative but to continue, and so with a sigh after a long and wistful look back to the east, he set forth to follow the sun.

"It was two more days before he reached the first slope which was grassy and easy to climb. There were rocks and boulders scattered about, but they represented no obstacle to First Cat. On the second day of his climb the grassland gave way to a forest of pine and fir trees, with sparse underbrush. The ground was covered with a bed of soft fragrant needles, making his travel easy. In the higher altitude he encountered some new species of creatures that he had never seen before, mostly birds, but as he broke through the forest's edge the next day, he met his first goats. It was cold, and the ground was partially covered by melting snow that had fallen the previous evening. Once again the terrain was mostly grass and boulders. Several goats were grazing nearby, and they looked at First Cat quizzically. First Cat approached cautiously. A large male goat placed himself between First Cat and the others. They sniffed noses. First Cat thought he had never encountered such a strong-smelling animal, and none too pleasant either. The goat thought there was a resemblance to his enemy, the cougar. It took a while, but at length they felt safe.

" 'Who are you?' Goat wanted to know. He had a strange nasal voice.

" 'I am First Cat. I come from Paradise, a land a long way off to the east.'

" 'Why do you travel so far from your home?' asked Goat.

"First Cat explained to Goat about his mission to save the world from the blight, and that he had to cross the mountains in order to continue to follow the sun. Goat introduced himself as a goat, a creature as at home in the mountains as the eagle is in the sky. He suggested that First Cat abandon his plan. 'You are not properly made to cross these mountains. The way is too rugged. The snow is too deep, the slope too steep, the air too thin. You will fall to your death or die from the cold,' said Goat.

" 'I cannot turn back,' First Cat said emphatically as he gazed up the steep slope. 'God has sent me, and everything depends upon my getting the crystal back to Paradise by the summer solstice. I have no time to go around these mountains.'

"Goat looked at First Cat for a long time, and realized that he would not heed the warning. He examined First Cat's coat and paws disapprovingly.

" 'If you must go on,' he said, 'we'll have to do something about your feet. Come with me.' He led First Cat to a cleft between two large boulders. In the cleft some bright yellow flowers grew up through fine powdery snow. 'Step into this cleft and stand in the snow by these flowers,' instructed Goat.

"First Cat cautiously obeyed. The snow barely covered his paws, which tingled in the cool wetness. He waited obediently until Goat gave him the sign that he could return into the open again. As he emerged from the cleft, he saw that his paws were now snow-white.

" 'Good,' said Goat as he sniffed at First Cat's magically transformed paws. 'From now on if you fall you will always land on your feet. This will be a blessing to you and to all your succeeding generations, because of your bravery and obedience to God's will. You will also notice that your toes are now webbed so that you will be able to walk through the snow. This is only a temporary change in your paws to help you during this stage of your quest. You will also need a guide to show you the way over the mountain. You will surely die if you don't know the way.'

"A nanny goat approached, and she and First Cat sniffed noses.

" 'Come,' she said, ' the way is difficult. We had better get started.'

"First Cat thanked him, and turned to follow his new guide. She nimbly loped and leapt up the steep mountainside, with First Cat struggling to keep up. Nanny Goat turned to look back, and saw that First Cat was making little progress. She scrambled back to where First Cat was trying to scale a rocky boulder-face. Nanny Goat watched with contempt.

" 'You can't climb this mountain!' she exclaimed. 'Just look at your feet!'

"First Cat looked at his white paws, and then at the goat's hooves. It was true that he wasn't getting any traction on the steep rocky slope, and Nanny was able to climb by jumping from place to place where she could balance herself. First Cat didn't have the strength to jump the way the goat could. They were both discouraged.

" 'Why don't you just give up and go home?' suggested Nanny. 'It is obvious that you can't climb this mountain.'

"First Cat sighed. He knew she was right. He didn't have the strength or the right kind of feet and legs for mountain climbing, even with the new magic Billy Goat had given him. He was discouraged, but having come this far he could not nor would not give up.

" 'Isn't there another way?' he inquired. 'Maybe we could find a path between two mountains.'

"Nanny stopped to consider. If Cat was determined to try, she would have to think of something. She did know of a pass between the mountains, but it was very dangerous, and she was none too interested in risking her own life. She lifted her head and sniffed at the wind. Snow was coming. If they were going to take the short-cut they would have to start immediately. If they waited it could be days or weeks before they could try again. She looked First Cat directly in his yellow eyes and saw the look of unrelenting determination. 'Cat,' she said, 'I do know another way, but it is very dangerous, and quite honestly, I think you'll probably get killed trying it. You decide, because I don't want to be responsible for your death. What you are trying isn't natural.' Most goats are not very spiritual, but it was obvious even to her that God never intended for cats to climb mountains.

" 'Lead the way,' said First Cat without hesitation. At that point he wasn't worried about danger. He was getting impatient to get on with his mission.

"He followed Nanny as she worked her way across the mountainside. They traveled for an hour or so. The going was difficult for First Cat, but at least it was a route that he could manage. Once he slipped and for a moment of terror he thought he was done for. As he fell through the air, though, he felt his body righting itself, and he landed on his paws a few feet below where he had lost his balance. He remained in a crouch for a few seconds while he tried to quickly assess his situation. Realizing that he was completely unhurt thanks to his new magic, he quickly scrambled back to where Nanny was disgustedly waiting for him.

" 'You'll have to be more careful, cat,' she said. ' This isn't going to get any easier.'

"First Cat wasn't sure that he could be any more careful, but he tried. He followed Nanny onto a rocky shelf that they followed until suddenly they were confronted with a sheer cliff. The shelf on which they traveled continued across the face of the cliff as far as he could see. The wind had picked up and was biting cold.

" 'Once we start across here there is no turning back,' warned Nanny. 'If you want to quit, now is the time to say so.'

"First Cat sniffed at the wind. It was cold, harsh, and unforgiving. Looking up, all he could see was the stone wall of the cliff, and looking down made him want to vomit.

" ' Don't look down, cat,' cautioned Nanny. 'It will make your head spin. As we proceed, you need to stay as close to the cliff as possible or a gust of wind might blow you right off the ledge. You also need to keep pace with me. We have to get to the other side before the storm hits or we'll be stranded up here and freeze to death.'

"She gave First Cat one last ominous look, but he gave no sign that he wanted to turn back. So they proceeded along the face of the cliff, Nanny leading Cat, with everything depending on their safe passage. They headed more or less into the wind, and First Cat discovered that if he did stay up with Nanny that she partially shielded him from its bite. They had proceeded a thousand or more feet with little difficulty when the ledge narrowed to no wider than First Cat himself. He fought off the obsessive urge to look down as he carefully but steadily followed Nanny. Now they were climbing some as the shelf became uneven for the first time. Sometimes it would widen a little, and at other times it was almost impossibly narrow. Suddenly Nanny hesitated as she came to a vertical crack in the face of the cliff. There was a gap in the ledge of about two feet, and the spot on the cliff-face where it picked up again was three or four feet below her. This was an easy leap for her, but she worried about First Cat. However, as they were fully committed to moving forward or dying, she jumped down and continued along the new ledge. There was not even enough room for her to look around to see if her companion had followed her, and the wind was now so high that she couldn't hear either. As First Cat reached the break in the ledge he also hesitated, but his fear of being left behind was greater than the fear of the jump. Actually, the jump was easy for a cat. It was only the thought of missing that was frightening. A few feet later, there was another break in the ledge, and so it went a couple of more times until once again they were on an even track along another broad cliff-face. It was getting colder, and a few snow flurries started to fly. The wind was high enough to blow the snow off the ledge, so at least for now, they didn't have the additional risk of the ledge being slippery. First Cat knew that wouldn't last forever, and he wondered how much further they would have to follow the shelf before they reached the pass. His paws were so cold that he could no longer feel them, and it was more of a struggle to keep up with Nanny. At last the cliff ended, and they were off the precipice. However, there was no time to relax.

" 'We have to find a cave before the storm gets too bad,' said Nanny as she turned back for a moment to assure herself that First Cat was still following her. He was too cold and emotionally exhausted to comment. He followed her over sharp rocks up a fairly steep grade. After what seemed like an eternity she led him into an opening in the side of the mountain. Suddenly they were out of the gale. Nanny explored the cavern quickly and cautiously to make sure they were alone. It was dark and quiet. First Cat sniffed around until he found a spot he felt satisfied with, and he fell asleep until the next day.

"When he awakened he did a little exploration. They were near the entrance, enough so that there was a little light. The cave was cold and dry. First Cat felt a sharp pain with each step of his right forepaw where he must have cut it on a sharp stone, and he licked the dried blood off. He was hungry. As he explored further he found Nanny, who he discovered, was also hungry, and in a bad mood.

" ' Good morning, Nanny,' he said. 'How do you feel?'

"Nanny glowered at him. 'How should I feel?' she replied. 'I'm hungry, I can't get back to my flock, and I'm trapped in a cave with a cat!'

" 'Can't we go?' inquired First Cat. He didn't realize they were trapped.

" ' Go look for yourself,' she answered.

" First Cat ventured forth to the mouth of the cave. A fierce storm raged outside. They would already be dead had Nanny not led them to the cave. There seemed to be no possibility of getting anything to eat.

" ' How long do you think we will be stuck here?' he asked.

" ' These spring storms don't last too long,' she replied. 'Probably we can continue in a day or two.'

" ' Maybe there is another way out of here,' he said, sniffing around.

" ' Don't be ridiculous, Cat,' said Nanny. 'Even if we did find another entrance instead of getting hopelessly lost, we'd still run into the same storm outside. Just make the best of it.' She turned away. She was hungry and completely out of sorts. She wanted to kick herself for letting herself get talked into this foolishness with this crazy cat on a crazy mission.

" Once First Cat accepted that he had no alternative, he was more relaxed about the whole thing. He realized that he had been so preoccupied that he had forgotten to pray or meditate, and even with the hunger in his belly and the aching of his paw, he now reflected on how much he had to be grateful for. After all, he was still alive, and he continued to make progress on his mission. He thought about the charms he had lost with regret at first, but upon further reflection, it occurred to him that probably he had needed them only to cross the river, and that each step of the way God would provide whatever he needed at that moment.

"All day and night they waited in the cave in silence, as Nanny had grown so resentful that she wouldn't talk. The following morning they ventured forth. The sun shone brightly on the gleaming snow which had drifted to great heights in some places while others were blown so clear that the goat was able to find a little something to graze on. First Cat had to wait patiently while she found a few mouthfuls of dried grass, and took her time about it too. He was weak with hunger and saw no sign of anything he could eat. At last they set forth in earnest. First Cat was amazed at the progress he made walking on the snow with his webbed paws. Their journey carried them between towering peaks, through rugged boulders, up and down steep inclines, until at around midday they suddenly emerged at the other side of the pass. First Cat looked out upon a splendid vista. Before him lay a glorious valley covered in a pristine blanket of sparkling white snow. Nanny led him down the other side of the mountain, and before dark they were beyond the snow. The earth was warmer, the grass was greener, and once again they were surrounded by the scents and sounds of spring. Somehow, First

Cat managed to find the energy to pounce on a sparrow that had carelessly strayed near him, and he and Nanny found cover for the night. She was very nervous, as she felt vulnerable without other goats to flock with. She would be easy prey for a mountain lion or wolves. The next day they were both able to eat well, and later in the afternoon they encountered another small group of goats. The Billy Goat came over and sniffed at her. She explained that she had come over the mountain with Cat, and didn't see how she was going to be able to return. Billy Goat approached First Cat warily, and after they sniffed at each other he made a threatening gesture causing First Cat to retreat hastily. Billy Goat kept himself between First Cat and the rest of the flock, and First Cat realized that he had lost his guide. He also realized that Billy was behaving according to his nature, and that the goats that had helped him must have been sent by God specifically to aid him in his quest. He tried to call after Nanny to thank her, but she was ignoring him as she grazed with her new flock; so he turned to continue down the mountain, and by late the next afternoon he could see in the distance a great forest.

"The sun was shining brightly as it crossed the sky heading towards its home in the West. First Cat found himself in a meadow beside a rushing, clear mountain stream. Wildflowers were in abundance, dazzling the eye with hues of red, gold, pale blue, and violet. The air was alive with the singing of birds, the buzzing of insects, and the happy burbling of the brook. For the first time in weeks, First Cat experienced relief from the constant tension of his dangerous journey as he frolicked in the meadow, leaping at butterflies, and rushing this way and that in the grass chasing God only knows what. As he rested later that evening, the sun long since having disappeared behind the dense forest, he gave thanks to God for getting him safely to this point on his mission. Who would have imagined that he could have safely crossed the mighty river, or more remarkably, the mountains? He realized that God was with him in his quest, and that if he failed it would not be because the task was too great, but because his fear was greater. He could not let himself be overpowered by his fear. He must remain prayerful, and confident in God's might and power to effect a righteous outcome to this great struggle. That night in his sleep a white buffalo calf came to him. It called him by a new name, Follows the Sun, and told him that from this time forth this was to be his name, because of his willingness to follow the sun on his sacred journey."

9

Amazing grace, how sweet the sound
That saved a wretch like me.
I once was lost, but now am found;
Was blind but now I see.

Talks with Wolves paused once again for a stretch, and I was ready for one myself. I liked First Cat's new name. It was more heroic, and a reminder that we all must follow the sun. I prowled aimlessly for a short while, and found myself behind Mrs. Baker's house. There was the clean, pungent odor of cedar in the air. I stretched out to groom myself, cleaning my fur with my rough tongue. My white paws gleamed in the moonlight, and I thought of Follows the Sun who had received the gift of the white paws from Goat. I felt connected to all things, and was at peace. After a few minutes I returned to our field just as Talks with Wolves was about to resume.

"Our ancestor has just received a new name in a dream from white buffalo calf, the Holy Spirit of God, as a reward for obedience to His will. Follows the Sun felt different with his new name, as one who has been given a great honor; and in the spirit of his own character, rather than feeling proud or arrogant, he was blessed with a deepened sense of humility and connectedness to God. He lay awake for a period of time thinking about what had transpired. He regretted that when he thought of what lay before him he was still afraid, but his success to this point, clearly not entirely the result of his own effort, gave him hope that God really was with him.

"He slept again and had another dream. Now he was visited by Kitouah, the nighthawk, who called him by his new name. 'Follows the Sun,' he said, 'you are about to enter a great forest. The trees are so tall that they reach nearly to the sky, and the overhead canopy is so dense that no light gets through, so that it is completely dark at all times. You will not be able to tell night from day. I have been sent to bestow a gift upon you, the gift of seeing in the dark. Come with me.'

"Follows the Sun followed Kitouah to a low hill nearby in a field devoid of trees. The moon was full and high, giving their surroundings an eerie glow.

" 'Look up at the moon,' commanded Kitouah. 'You must keep your gaze focused on the moon until I tell you that you may look away. As you stare at the moon I will fly around it many times. If you do not break your concentration you and all your subsequent generations will have night vision, the moonlight being in your eyes.'

"Without another word Kitouah silently flew into the sky. Follows the Sun looked up at the bright full moon which seemed to fill the sky with light. As he stared intently at it he could see the shadow of Kitouah, circling slowly at first, and calling out with his characteristic short note. As Follows the Sun stared, the bird circled faster and faster, calling out more and more rapidly, until he flew around the moon so fast that he was just a blur, his call a rapid staccato. As he did so the moon grew brighter and brighter, and larger and larger, until it was as though it filled the sky with its brilliance. Follows the Sun was in a trance and lost track of time, but suddenly Kitouah was next to him again. He looked around when he was given permission, in astonishment. He could see every blade of grass clearly, as though it was a bright sunny day. The only difference was that there was no color, only shades of gray. Kitouah was now clearly visible in all his detail (but still a very plain bird).

" ' Thank you, Kitouah, this is a wonderful and remarkable gift you have given me,' said Follows the Sun. 'Now I shall be able to see my way through the great forest.'

" ' Do not thank me,' replied Kitouah, 'I have done only as God has bidden me. Use your gift well.'

"With that he flew away, and not long thereafter, Follows the Sun awakened. It was a bright moonlit night, but at once he was amazed by the clarity of his vision. He could see nearly as well as in daylight, except for there being no color. He wondered if he was still dreaming. After sniffing around for a few minutes he stopped to groom himself briefly, and then meditated. He realized that he had yet another gift from God to help him in his quest. First there was the pouch given him by Hawk. This had given him the magic he had needed to get across the river without drowning. Next there was the transformation of his paws from Goat so that he could safely cross the mountains. And now this. He once again gave thanks to God for being with him at all times. Emerging from his meditation he stretched. Hunger was in his belly, and he prepared to hunt. He had a feeling he would need to be well fed and rested before he ventured into the forest that morning.

"With the sun rising behind him, Follows the Sun took a deep breath and entered the great forest. He was at once astonished by the size of the trees, and the extent of the darkness. It was as dark in the forest as the darkest night. The canopy of leaves at the roof of the forest was so dense, that it admitted no sunlight, and without the new gift of seeing in the dark, Follows the Sun would have been as one who is blind. Even so, he could see little more than the shadowy shapes of huge tree trunks. He sniffed around at the forest floor. There was something very strange. Everything smelled the same. The only odor was the leaf mold of the forest floor. He detected no trace of animal life, no herbs, ferns, or plants of any kind.

" 'Of course,' he thought, 'there is no light here for plants to grow, and nothing for the little animals to eat.'

"Follows the Sun remembered that Hawk had warned him of dangerous dogs and bears, so he assumed that there must be something to eat somewhere in the forest. He proceeded cautiously. The terrain was quite flat, and the going was easy, the huge trees being well-spaced and there being nothing else to impede his progress. The ground was dry, as no rain was able to penetrate the canopy either. Every so often, though, he came to a small stream where he was able to drink water. He wondered how the trees survived without rain, but since there were streams he concluded that there must be an underground source of water. Now and then he would stop and listen intently, but could hear nothing other the sound of his own breathing. It was so quiet that he thought he could even hear his heart beating. He continued on for what he assumed was the better part of the day. Without any hint of where the sun was, he had no visual cue for the passage of time, but as hungry as he had become, he knew he had walked for several hours. He also was aware that unless he continued in a straight line, he would have no idea of direction, and he would be hopelessly lost. He was even afraid to stop and nap because of his concern about becoming disoriented. The forest looked the same in every direction, so if he didn't wake up pointed exactly the same way as when he fell asleep, he would have no means of knowing which way to go, and of course, he wouldn't know if he had changed position or not. He couldn't even be absolutely certain that he hadn't already gotten off course, as he did have to change direction enough to walk past trees directly in his path. No idea came to him other than to keep going in as straight a line as he could, which he did for several more hours. Just as he thought that he would be unable to stay awake another minute he stopped to sniff and listen again, and for the first time he heard something. At first the sound was so distant as to be unrecognizable, but it grew louder, and as it did so, Follows the Sun bristled with fear. What he heard was the baying and bellowing of a pack of hounds, and he had no doubt that they were coming his way. If they hadn't picked up his scent already, they soon would.

"Follows the Sun began to move quickly in the opposite direction as quietly as possible so as not to attract their attention in case they had not become aware of his presence. But each time he stopped to listen, they grew louder. Soon it was obvious that they had a bead on him and were closing in quickly. Follows the Sun broke into a dead run through the woods just as the hounds came into sight. He darted this way and that as he felt their hot breath on him and their jaws snapping at his heels. Then his instincts took over and he shot up a tree trunk several feet above where the hounds were circling and barking. They jumped as high as they could, but he had stopped safely above their reach. Follows the Sun clung to the side of the tree feeling momentarily safe, and he surveyed his situation. Looking up, he saw no branches coming off the trunk so there would be no comfortable place to stretch out and rest. He could climb higher but there was no telling how high he would have to go, as the tree trunks disappeared into the darkness above. Climbing down was certainly out of the question. He could do nothing but wait and hope that the dogs would get bored and move on.

"Having lost track of time, he could only guess, but what seemed to him to be several hours later the only change was that the dogs weren't quite so frenzied in their leaping and barking. He didn't think he could hold on much longer. He hadn't eaten or slept in probably over a day. His muscles were aching from grasping the tree for hours on end. Desperately he prayed that God rescue him from his predicament. Several more hours passed.

Follows the Sun would doze off and then awaken with a start as he felt his grip relax, be wide-awake and in agony for several minutes, and then doze off again. Just as he was as close to giving up hope as he had ever been, the dogs became wild again. Glancing down, Follows the Sun saw that an enormous bear had come along, evidently attracted by the commotion. The dogs mobbed him, growling, leaping, barking, and biting. The bear had reared up on his hind legs and was slashing at the dogs with his powerful fore paws. As determined as the frustrated hounds were, they were no match for the bear. Two or three of them were killed outright, being slashed open by his sharp claws. Several others were seriously injured, and suddenly off they ran, baying and yelping into the distance.

"The bear sat down and began to lick his wounds. He sniffed at the dead dogs and rolled them over, making sure they would be no more trouble. As he looked around he suddenly caught sight of Follows the Sun who had witnessed the entire spectacle with terrified fascination. With one remarkably quick motion the bear rose on his hind legs, growled, and took a swipe with his right forepaw at Follows the Sun who was only barely out of reach. Quickly, he scurried up the tree several more feet, and looked down in horror as the bear wrapped himself around the base of the trunk and began to climb. Farther up the tree went Follows the Sun, with the bear following relentlessly. Follows the Sun tried to think through his fear and exhaustion. It was possible that if he climbed high enough the bear would give up. This seemed to be an undependable solution, especially since the bear was gaining on him, being a more expert climber. Turning and fighting was a joke. The only advantage he would have would be the element of surprise, but it seemed foolish. He could try to rush past the bear on the other side of the trunk, but the bear was pretty well wrapped around it, and all it would take was one swipe and Follows the Sun would be cut in two. He looked around. No other tree was close enough for him to jump. He climbed several more feet ahead of the bear and stopped to nervously groom himself, as we all sometimes do. As he did so he noticed his white paws and remembered the gift he had received from Goat. He guessed that he was now forty or fifty feet off the ground and felt fear rise within him at the prospect of falling such a great distance. But just as the bear was about to reach him and slash him to ribbons, he summoned his last ounce of strength and pushed himself away from the trunk, leaving the astonished bear slashing at nothing at all.

"If Follows the Sun had given himself much time to think he may never have jumped. As he fell he felt his body righting itself, and before he had too much time to worry about not knowing how to land, he landed on the soft forest floor. He took a few seconds to come to his senses. His body ached and he was exhausted, but he quickly realized that he was uninjured from the fall. He groomed himself briefly and looked up at the tree. Even with the moonlight in his eyes, the bear was too high for him to make out clearly. Quickly he made his way away from there hoping that the bear wouldn't follow him, and that the dogs were long gone. Follows the Sun forced himself to push ahead through his exhaustion, fearing that the danger wasn't yet over. Finally, he started to look for cover so he could sleep. But there was no cover, only huge tree trunks and a forest floor of leaf mold. He stopped for a moment to consider what he should do, and the next thing he knew he was waking up after what seemed like the deepest, longest sleep of his lifetime.

"He awakened to an unpleasant reality. He felt weak and hungry, ached all over, and was hopelessly lost. He had no clue about finding his way or about finding something to eat. About all he had accomplished to this point was to avoid being killed by the dogs or the bear. He stood up and stretched, and then sniffed around. Everything smelled the same. It was extremely dark and even with his night vision he could only see a few tree trunks in any direction. He pricked up his ears as he thought he heard something, and then he smelled something familiar. At first he wasn't sure, but after a few minutes he smelled it again, and more strongly this time. It was the last thing he expected to encounter in this forest, and despite his debilitated state, he felt aroused. He followed the scent, and before long he saw her. She was a long-haired, white, fairly large cat, so white that she seemed to glow in the moonlight of his eyes. And she was in heat. They approached and sniffed at each other, and before long they mated. Follows the Sun was astonished by the power he felt in her loins, and overcome by her beauty. The experience was almost surreal, there in the dark-as-night forest, mating with this exotic female who seemed to give off her own soft light. As he finished she turned on him in the way of females, snarled, and raked at him with her forepaw, cutting into the flesh just above his shoulder. The ferocity of her attack caught him by surprise, and he retreated a short distance to lick his wound and groom himself. Soon they were sniffing at each other again, and the female spoke.

" 'I am Delilah,' she said. 'I know who you are and why you are here. I have been sent to guide you through the woods, just as Otter helped you cross the river, and Goat helped you to cross the mountains.'

" 'I am grateful for your assistance,' replied Follows the Sun. 'I am completely lost and terribly hungry. You are strong and well-fed. Please take me to where I may hunt.'

" ' Of course,' answered Delilah, 'but there is nothing for a cat to eat in this part of the forest. You must follow me. I will lead you to good hunting grounds.'

"Follows the Sun did follow her as she made her way through the dark woods. Several more times they mated, and each time her post-coital attack was more fierce, but he was wary and managed to not get wounded again. However, the matings sapped what little strength he had left. They traveled a long way until she announced that they could stop and rest. The terrain had changed somewhat. The ground was uneven and boulders of various sizes were scattered about. The trees, though, were just as large, and there was no more light than before. And there was still nothing to eat.

" 'We can stop here to sleep,' instructed Delilah, leading the way into a narrow cleft between some large boulders.

"Follows the Sun obeyed, and they huddled together among the rocks and slept. It seemed colder as they huddled there. One thing he had been grateful for was a comfortable temperature, as he had been so cold through his two previous challenges. As he lay there next to her he realized that in fact she was colder than he was, and upon reflection, he had noticed this each time they had mated. He speculated that it might have to do with the moon-glow light she gave off. But he was extremely weak, tired, and hungry, and didn't dwell on this peculiarity of Delilah's.

" 'When may I eat?' he asked. "I don't think I can go on much longer.'

" 'We come to the hunting grounds tomorrow,' she responded. 'Then we can both fill our stomachs. For now you need to sleep.'

"Follows the Sun quickly gave in to his exhaustion, and slept for a long time. When he awakened he saw that Delilah had climbed up onto a nearly boulder and was resting there. He sniffed the air, realized that her time had passed to be in heat, and breathed a sigh of relief. They drank water from a nearby stream and continued on their way. It was another long trek during which the terrain grew more rugged, but nothing else changed. There was no sign of animal life anywhere, and the only plant life was the giant trees

73

that choked out everything else. He was faint with hunger and had little strength to continue, but she urged him along with the promise that they would eat soon.

"After a long day's journey they stopped to rest again. It suddenly struck him as strange that Delilah did not appear to be weakening. Although he had lost track of time he guessed that he hadn't eaten for at least three days. He had been with her for about a day, during which she had not eaten; and she couldn't have eaten just before he encountered her because there was no food anywhere nearby. Surely, if food was available to her, he would have had a chance to eat by now. So it was perplexing to him how she could appear to be so strong while he was so weak.

"They continued onward, and the way became more treacherous. She led him to the edge of a ravine and they traveled along it for some time. Without his night vision he would certainly have mis-stepped and fallen. Delilah had made her way quite a bit ahead of Follows the Sun as he carefully picked his way along the rocky edge of the ravine. Eventually she stopped and he caught up with her.

" 'You are weaker than I had realized,' she said. 'We won't make it to the hunting grounds today. We will stop here and sleep under the cover of these boulders.'

"Follows the Sun stared at her for a few moments, and then without a word fell over on his side, exhausted. He fell into a deep sleep, and as he did so he dreamed. In his dream he was in an open field. The sun shone brightly on a warm day. He chased butterflies happily, and then lay in the warmth of the sun, grooming himself. He heard a cry of distress. It was the nanny goat who had helped him cross the mountain. She needed his help urgently. Quickly he went in the direction of her call, but after a while he found himself exactly at the place from which he had started. Now she called from a different direction and he ventured forth, only to arrive back at his starting point some time later. Time and time again she called, and always he wound up where he had started, never getting even close to her.

"He awakened from the dream feeling deeply troubled, and considered his situation. He was lost and dependent entirely on Delilah to lead him out of the woods. Not only was there no evidence of progress, but she had not even found food for him, and had led him to the edge of a dangerous ravine where in his weakened state he could have easily fallen. She was strangely cold, and seemed none the worse for not having eaten. He thought back to what seemed a very long time previously when Hawk had spoken to him.

" 'You will meet many in your travels who will help you,' Hawk had said, 'but beware, for there will also be those who will try to deceive you.'

"Follows the Sun continued to lie on his side, pretending to be asleep while he did his best to decide what he needed to do. He prayed to God for wisdom and guidance. Was Delilah his enemy, or was he imagining things in his debilitated state? What could he do about it if she was an enemy of his mission? Could he afford to not do something now, considering that if he had to go another day without food he would be too weak to have any hope of defending himself? These were his thoughts on that morning as he realized that his mission was in great danger. Slowly he stirred, stood up, stretched, and sauntered over to where she was resting. As he drew very near to her, her ears pricked up and her long white fur started to rise.

"Follows the Sun lunged at her, trying to force his fangs into her throat, but her fur was too thick. She broke loose from his grasp and promptly attacked him. Her strength was overwhelming. She took a powerful hold on his undersides with her claws as she bit into his throat. He grappled back as best he could as they rolled over and over. A frightening yowl emitted from her throat as she pressed her death grip forward. Follows the Sun saw that they were near the edge of the ravine, and with his last particle of strength he lurched his body towards it. Delilah was so preoccupied with his throat that she didn't realize the danger, and suddenly they were hurtling through the air over the edge of the precipice. Startled, she lifted her head to look, and when she did, Follows the Sun kicked her ribs as hard as he could with his hind legs, breaking her grip. Once free from her hold, his body righted itself as he continued to fall, but she tumbled head over heels, and when they landed he was on his feet, and she landed next to him on her side.

"They had fallen quite a distance, but once again Follows the Sun quickly realized that he wasn't injured. He sniffed at Delilah. She was stunned and not moving, but she was alive, and probably would recover quickly. He knew he had to kill her, and once again tried to bury his fangs in her throat. Once again, her fur was too thick. She began to stir and opened her eyes. As her consciousness began to return, Follows the Sun opened his jaws wide and clamped them down directly over her face, covering her mouth and nose with his mouth. Now she was fully alert and tried to stand up and shake him off. Her strength was enormous as she tossed her head this way and that, lifting Follows the Sun completely off the ground as she did so. She dug her front claws into his face and kicked furiously, raking his belly with her hind claws. Desperately she struggled to break his grip so that she could breathe, and just as desperately, he held his mouth clamped shut over her nose and mouth, disregarding the intense pain she was inflicting on him. The battle of wills continued, the struggle to kill or be killed, and then suddenly it was over. After a last convulsive kick, Delilah went limp.

"Follows the Sun didn't let go for a long time, but finally was convinced that he had prevailed, and he relaxed his grip on her face. He moved a few yards away, and began to lick his numerous wounds. He had never been in so much pain. He had so many injuries that he couldn't even tell where he hurt, and he was even more mentally and physically exhausted. As he licked himself he remembered to thank God for once again being with him, and as he was so engaged, a remarkable thing happened. The glow of Delilah's fur had disappeared when she died, but now she was glowing more brightly than ever, and as Follows the Sun watched in amazement, a glowing ethereal being rose from her corpse which itself remained motionless. Gradually the being took form, until a human female stood before him. She picked him up and carried him to a nearby stream where she washed his fur and cleaned out his cuts. She took a sharp stone and dug into the earth until she uncovered a root. Grinding the root between two stones and adding water, she made a paste which she applied to his wounds . Taking the sharp stone again, she cut a lock of her long black hair, fashioned it into a snare, and went back to the stream. She crouched quietly by the stream, lowered the snare into the water, and a few moments later had a small fish in her hands that he gratefully ate. She then lay him down on some soft leaf mold, and sat by him while he slept."

10

Go down, Moses, way down in Egypt land;
Tell old Pharaoh, let My people go.

Talks with Wolves rolled over on his back and began what looked as
though it was to be a thorough washing of himself. Needing a good break
myself, I got up and stretched luxuriously first my forelimbs and then
my hind legs. That felt excellent, and relieved some of the tension that
had built up as I heard the story. Even though I had heard it many times
before, I always got into the drama as I identified with Follows the Sun on
his heroic journey. Grits followed me as I wandered away, idly sniffing at
this and that. We made our way into someone's front yard and lay beneath
a nandina shrub. Everything was quiet on that bright moonlit night. Grits
was in deep thought as she reflected on what she had heard thus far.
   "You have white paws just like Follows the Sun," she said.
   "As do you," I replied.
   "Yes," she said.
   There was a long silence during which I did some grooming of myself,
and then of her. We could hear a freight train in the distance, and I thought
of my fateful ride with the hobo many years previously, so far in the distant
past that it seemed like a different lifetime. Life had been good to me, and
like the hero in the tale, God had always provided me with what I needed at
the time. The white of Grits's fur seemed to glow in the moonlight and I
couldn't help but think how beautiful she was, tail or no tail. I was grateful
she was still in my life.
   "Tell me about Delilah," she said, looking troubled.
   "She represents the evil inclination," I replied. "We are all capable of
being led down the wrong path. Sometimes that which looks right and

wonderful can in truth be just the opposite."

"But how can we tell whether a thing is right or wrong?" she inquired.

"At first we may be deceived. We all will be misled at times even when we want to do right, and want to please God. But if we remain prayerful and look within ourselves, eventually we will know the truth. The tree can be told by the fruit it bears. And once we discover our error we must act to correct our mistake."

"So his attack on her was indicative of what I must do if I have wandered from my spiritual path?" she asked.

"Yes," I answered. "We have to face our fears squarely. We can't do it without God's help, but neither will He do it for us. There are times when we either take action or fall by the wayside."

"What about the woman?" asked Grits. "What does she represent?"

"Nature cannot tolerate a spiritual vacuum. When evil energy is eliminated the space is filled with good," I replied. "We grow along spiritual lines by confronting what is wrong within ourselves and in the world around us."

We were silent once more for a few moments. A bat fluttered silently by, seeking its nocturnal nourishment.

"I think you are the most handsome cat I have ever seen," Grits suddenly blurted out.

If cats could blush, I would have. Without another word we made our way back to the gathering where Talks with Wolves was once again preparing to continue his tale.

"So Follows the Sun was in a severely debilitated state, and the woman gradually nursed him back to health. She brought him little fishes to eat, and applied balm to his wounds. She even sang to him, and danced, a graceful shadowy form creating a healing energy that bathed him in its wake. At last, he knew it was time to continue his quest. He didn't feel completely well, but was strong enough to proceed, and if he could find food he would continue to gain strength. She led him through the woods another three days journey, by his estimate. They passed by several bears on the way, but the bears ignored them. Follows the Sun hoped there would be no more dogs. He didn't think he could tolerate another such experience.

"And then suddenly they emerged from the forest into bright sunlight.

He had been in the deep darkness for so long that his eyes burned with the light and he shut them tightly, briefly opening them every few minutes until at last he adjusted. Looking around, he found himself in a lush meadow by a pond. Water lilies floated on the quiet pond as dragonflies skimmed the surface, hovering and darting this way and that. A small herd of buffalo grazed nearby, seemingly unaware of the newcomers. Many familiar scents came to Follows the Sun as he sniffed about, exploring his new world somewhat tentatively. It was as though he had emerged from the bowels of Hell itself, and had been reborn. He grew bolder and moved towards the herd, encountering piles of fresh manure lying amongst the grass, daisies, and purple coneflowers. He was back in a living world, and it was good. As Follows the Sun explored, his thoughts once again turned to his mission. He had lost track of time, but thought he had little to waste.

"A large male approached him and they touched noses. The woman stood next to the buffalo and rubbed his head.

" ' This is Follows the Sun,' she said to Buffalo. 'He must reach the castle that lies three days journey from here. Can you help him?'

"The bull turned his head to the west and gazed across the meadow thoughtfully, flicking his tail at the flies that were the only annoyance of his otherwise blissful existence. He looked at the cat and spoke in a deep voice.

" ' Others have come before you,' he said. He gazed back to the west, and then turned back to Follows the Sun. 'Maybe this time it will be different. I sense a powerful energy surrounding you. Come with me.'

"Follows the Sun followed the huge animal a short distance to where some cows were lying with their calves, all chewing their cuds. They approached a white calf with large soft brown eyes. It was the same calf of his dream.   Follows the Sun touched noses with White Buffalo Calf. She had the sweetest scent he had ever imagined. He felt the warmth of her breath on his face. Slowly she sniffed at him, and then methodically she licked him all over. Her tongue was soft and warm, the strokes strong and gentle at the same time. As she covered him with her sweetness he felt himself glowing within, a swelling ecstasy of joy filling his being. He knew that the Spirit of God had entered him, and that he need never be fearful again. At length she stopped, turned to the cow lying next to her, and began to nurse.

" 'Now nothing can stop you,' said Buffalo. 'There are yet many dangers, but God is with you. Go!'

"With that, the bull returned to his grazing. Follows the Sun looked around. The woman was gone. Turning his back to the dense forest from which he had so recently emerged, he headed west across the meadow. The hunting was excellent and there was plenty of cover for two days. On the third day the ground became rather boggy, and it was more difficult going. Mud turned to muck as the stench of swamp filled his nostrils. He circled the edge of the bog and managed to make his way through surprisingly well. He encountered wild pigs and crocodiles, giving them a wide berth. There were water snakes as well. Using much caution, he managed to pass safely unnoticed by these dangerous creatures for a great distance. At times he had to swim past huge cypress trees growing in the standing water. He spent the night in a large hollow log, near an opossum family who tolerated his presence, much to his surprise.

"In the gray light of morning, as he continued on his way, he heard a familiar, yet terrible sound. It was a pack of dogs, and they were coming his way. As quickly as he could, he moved forward, the barking growing louder and louder. The terrain remained swampy and difficult, but just as the dogs were almost upon him he broke into a large clearing, possibly one hundred yards square. Without taking any time to think, he dashed into the clearing, his white paws barely touching the damp sandy soil, and raced the full length of it, not stopping until he reached the other side. And the strangest thing happened as he raced across. The dogs immediately behind him quickly became stuck. The next group of dogs entered the clearing and made more progress, racing across the backs of the sinking dogs. Before any of them could react, all the dogs found themselves in quicksand. God had made Follows the Sun's body touch the ground so lightly as he sped across that he didn't sink into the mire. But the large and heavy dogs became entrapped, and as Follows the Sun watched from the opposite side, they sank amidst howls and yelps of terror and rage, until suddenly it was deathly silent. Then came the powerful swell of a joyful chorus of birds and frogs, as though they were angels singing. And in the midst of this joyful profusion of sound, Follows the Sun spoke, saying:

'Let us sing a new song of thanks to God;
To Him all praise is due.
For He has delivered us from our enemies,

And brought us safely to the shore.
He has cast the dogs into the mire,
And smashed the forces of evil.
He has given us feet of snow,
And caused moonlight to dwell in our eyes.
Through His servant, White Buffalo Calf,
He has caused His Holy Spirit to dwell within us.
He has brought us across a mighty river;
Over great mountains has He led us.
He brought us through the forest of Hell,
And delivered us from the forces of evil.
He sent the woman to heal our wounds,
And to lead us to safety.
Yes, now we know that God is with us;
He is our Rock and our Shield.
He is our Saving Power.
How can we fail in our journey
When God is with us?
Joyfully shall we proceed to do His work
And dwell in His fields forever.'

"And having thus uttered his hymn of praise, Follows the Sun turned to continue on his way. It was only a few more minutes until he once again came to a meadow, across which in the distance he saw a great castle.

"Follows the Sun had never seen a castle before. In fact, when Hawk had told him the crystal was being held in the highest tower of a castle, he hadn't exactly understood what that meant. But when he saw the great castle in the distance he knew immediately what it was. He was too far to fully take it in, but it was an awesome sight, a stone fortress with many turrets, towers, and parapets. The terrain was quite flat, with grassy meadows and cultivated fields forming a patchwork of green and gold. The castle was on the highest elevation in the area, but for all that, not on what you would call a hill. Follows the Sun approached cautiously, sniffing his way through fields of corn, wheat, and alfalfa. He encountered clusters of buildings where he found many unfamiliar scents, animals he had never before encountered: ducks, chickens, geese, and horses. He found sheep and cattle grazing in grassy fields. Strange smells came from some of the buildings, and he saw smoke rising from a chimney. Still wary, he approached one house, and spotted a dog asleep in the yard. Keeping downwind, he worked his way carefully past the house, only to encounter a big tabby cat. They hissed at each other and bared their teeth. Follows the Sun kept moving, working his way carefully towards the castle.

"He was in better physical condition than he had been in for a long time, but still not completely fit. He recalled that Hawk had told him the only creature who had reached the castle was Man, but that he had still failed in his mission. He knew that great danger and difficulty lay ahead of him, and he wanted to be in the best possible condition, mentally, physically, and spiritually. So he took no chances and avoided unnecessary scrapes with dogs or cats. He approached another farm. A lady was standing in front of her house throwing fistfuls of corn to some chickens that fluttered about her as they clucked and squawked in a most disagreeable fashion. He was struck by what he thought was her strange fur, as the few humans he had encountered up to that time had not worn clothes. She gently scolded the chickens as she fed them, telling them how unmannerly they were, and how embarrassed their mothers would be if they knew how rudely and greedily they behaved. Follows the Sun came into the yard, feeling an instinctive attraction to her. Cats have always had the instinctive ability to know which people are most deeply instilled with God's gift of wanting to love and care for us. As he approached the woman the chickens scattered in a small cloud of dust and feathers. He rubbed against her legs, walking back and forth, looking up at her and also keeping an eye out for other cats or a dog which might wander by.

" 'Hello, kitty,' said the woman. 'You're a new kitty here, aren't you? And what a handsome cat-boy you are, too!'

"She turned and went into the house, Follows the Sun at her heels. It was quite dark in the house, the only light coming in through the open door, and through one small window. It was sparsely furnished with a bed, table, two chairs, and a hutch where she kept her few dishes and utensils. Pots hung near a large fireplace where embers smoldered, giving off a pungent aroma of wood smoke and bacon. A door led to a storeroom where she kept her provisions: cornmeal, flour, potatoes, and other foodstuffs. He followed her into the storeroom where she had a pail of fresh milk.

" 'Aren't you the nosiest cat-boy I have ever seen?' she scolded. He followed her back into the living space where she poured some milk into a small bowl and placed it on the dirt floor for him. Eagerly he lapped at it, thinking that it was the most wonderful food he had ever encountered, except for mice, of course. Shortly the milk was gone, and he was busy exploring, jumping up first on the hutch, then the mantel, and in no time had made himself completely at home. The woman put up her milk pail and sat down in her chair. Follows the Sun jumped into her lap and settled into a lovely nap, as she talked to him softly and stroked his fur. After his nap he jumped onto her bed and groomed himself thoroughly. Later that evening he explored the small farmyard. There was a chicken coop, a pig pen, and a small barn where she kept a few cows and a mule. A shed contained some tools. It was a great place for a cat. The mousing was terrific, and the woman was most loving. He would spend a few days here, he decided, before he tried to figure out how to get into the castle. He spent part of the night in the woman's house, curled up next to her on her pillow. He had to get a little rough with another cat who tried to encroach on his space, provoking more gentle scolding from the woman.

"The mule proved to be interesting company. They took walks together and got acquainted. Mule explained that he had to work only a few days a year, pulling a plow, in exchange for his stable and food. He had been there many years, enjoying his life. He told him the woman's husband had died before she had children, and that this was what gave her such a capacity for loving her animals. She was almost completely self-sufficient, needing help only with the plowing and harvesting. She had a special magnetism for cats. She called them all by pet names and sang them little songs. She had a couple of apathetic dogs who seemed to serve no purpose whatsoever, but at least they didn't bother the other animals.

"It wasn't long before he and the other cats had established their rules of conduct and learned to tolerate each other. He was totally ignored by the cows, the ducks and chickens gave him a wide berth, he gave the geese a wide berth, and amazingly, he started hanging out some with the dogs. He spent parts of each night sleeping with the woman, but liked to go in and out of the house several times, so he could hunt and explore. Soon the woman was calling him Mister White Paws, and he felt entirely at home with her. Days turned into weeks in this blissful existence, and the truth of the matter is, that he kind of forgot that he was in reality Follows the Sun, and that God had sent him on a vital mission. But he regained all his lost weight, and was certainly well-rested, strong, and healthy.

"It was well into springtime. The air hung sweetly with the aroma of freshly-mown alfalfa, and Follows the Sun napped in the front yard with the dogs on a warm afternoon. As he slept he dreamed a dream in which he was walking through the fields near the woman's home. He had a sense of grim foreboding, as he noticed small brown spots on the corn leaves. The edges of the leaves also were curling inward slightly. In the alfalfa field the bales were covered with sour-smelling black slime. Large black flies flew around the eyes of the animals, vexing them greatly. A lamb lay sick in the pasture, and vultures circled overhead. The grass was dry, brown, and brittle under Follows the Sun's paws as he sniffed at the lamb which was bleating pitifully. A ewe looked at him with large, sad, accusing brown eyes. Follows the Sun awakened with a start.

"As he looked around he saw the dogs still sleeping. A few chickens were at the edge of the yard, pecking at the ground and keeping their distance. The ground was dusty as it hadn't rained for several days. Follows the Sun stretched, and then nervously groomed himself, as we all do when we feel stress. He realized that he had become so comfortable that he had forgotten about what God had sent him to do. He had become negligent about his prayer and meditation, being perfunctory with it, or even forgetting it altogether. He was astonished at how quickly he could have become so diverted from his path. Looking up at the cloudless sky he saw there were several more hours of daylight left. It was time to have a better look at the castle. He wandered into the barn where the Mule was eating hay.

" 'Let's go for a walk,' he said to Mule, 'I haven't had a good look at the castle since I've been here.'

" ' Okay,' replied Mule, and the two of them walked down a narrow path, Mule leading the way. The path had been made by deer as they traversed the edge of the field on their way to a stream, which on that day was easy to cross as it hadn't rained. Before long, after cutting through a wooded glen, they emerged onto the vast grassy plain where the castle sat, surrounded by a moat.

" ' This is close enough,' said Mule. 'We don't want to be noticed.'

" 'Why not?' asked Follows the Sun.

" ' The castle is owned by an evil witch, and guarded by fierce monsters,' replied Mule. 'What is the sense of asking for trouble?'

"They were both silent as they stood there gazing at the impressive fortress. It had massive stone walls that rose far into the sky. A moat completely surrounded the castle. From where they stood they could see an enormous door that stood directly behind a drawbridge. Mule explained how the drawbridge worked, and that it was always up unless the door opened to let people in or out. He also commented that many more people went in than ever came out. It was rumored that she kept slaves, that she had a terrible dungeon where people were kept for years, and that she ate cats and dogs. Follows the Sun shuddered. He had never heard of anything so horrible. He looked at the castle. A tower stood at each corner, and the tower closest to them was clearly the tallest. A tiny slit of a window could be seen.

" 'I wonder how I could get in,' said Follows the Sun with studied nonchalance. He wasn't ready to let anyone in on his secret.

" 'Getting in wouldn't be a problem,' sneered Mule. 'Getting out would be the problem. To get in all you would need to do is wait until they lower the bridge, walk across, and announce that you are there for the witch's breakfast.' He shook his head and glowered at Cat. 'What kind of an idiotic question is that?'

" 'Oh, I was just wondering,' replied Follows the Sun. 'I mean, I've never been in a castle before. Maybe I could sort of sneak in.'

" 'Never!' exclaimed Mule emphatically. 'The witch has evil monsters that are on constant patrol inside. In fact, I'm pretty sure we are under surveillance right now, as far as we are from the castle.'

" 'I see,' said Follows the Sun. 'Let me jump up for a better look.'

"Before Mule knew what happened, Follows the Sun had jumped up on his back, and run up his neck to stand on his head.

" 'Hey!' exclaimed the startled Mule. 'Watch the claws!'

"Before long Mule got too nervous and turned away from the castle and back into the wooded glen.

" 'You've got to be more careful,' he said. 'If anyone was watching, that stunt would have definitely attracted way too much attention.'

"Follows the Sun jumped down and they walked back to the farm in silence. He absentmindedly caught a mouse in the barn and ate it, his mind very much elsewhere. The woman had prepared her own dinner and he went inside to see what treat she might have in store for him. After dinner she went back outside to finish her chores while Follows the Sun curled up in front of the fireplace and groomed himself. He waited for a plan to form in his mind. Then he waited some more. No plan made its appearance. It seemed too dangerous to enter the castle, and the only other access to the tower was a slit of a window high in the air, in a sheer stone wall, making it appear quite inaccessible. The woman returned to the cabin, sat in her chair, and took up her knitting. Follows the Sun jumped into her lap and nuzzled her breast.

" 'What's the matter, Mister White Paws?' she said. 'Aren't you going to try to play with my yarn? You must be very tired. Did you have a busy day?'

"Follows the Sun rested quietly in her lap, purring softly. He had found such a pleasant home, and wished he didn't have to leave. It was getting fairly late in the spring, and he didn't suppose he had a lot of time to dawdle. And there was another thing that had been nagging at him for a while, but each time it rose in his consciousness, he suppressed it. What was he going to do with the crystal even if he did get hold of it? He had no idea how to get back to Paradise. He certainly had no intention of going back the way he came! He decided he would deal with that problem when he was confronted with it.

"The woman got ready for bed and went to sleep. Follows the Sun went outside in the cool dry night. He found himself retracing his steps back to the edge of the wooded glen across the field from the castle. The night was very dark with only a sliver of a moon in a black sky blazing with stars. Slowly, he crossed the field and approached the moat. He carefully circled it, examining every blade of grass. Quietly, he lowered himself into the still water and swam to the other side. Climbing out on the other side, he cautiously explored the base of the castle. He was frightened about the possibility of being detected, but he had to know as much as he could about what he was dealing with, and to look for any possible ways to get in other than the front door. When he arrived back at the farm with the first gray light of dawn he brought with him the glimmer of an idea.

11

> He's got the whole world, in His Hand,
> He's got the whole wide world, in His Hand,
> He's got the whole world, in His Hand,
> He's got the whole world in His Hand.

"Follows the Sun slept late the following morning prompting more fussing by the woman.

" 'Why you lazy Mister White Paws,' she scolded. 'You're sleeping so late, you're letting all the best mice get away!'

"He went outside and entered the barn, having decided to take Mule into his confidence. He felt that he could trust him. Mule had been around for a long time, and knew the area as well as anyone. He also seemed to know a lot about the witch and her habits. Anyway, Mule was by far the smartest animal around, even smarter than the pigs, and he needed to take advantage of his intelligence. They talked quietly for a long time. It was Mule's opinion that Follows the Sun was a nut case. On the other hand, everyone feared and hated the witch, and if they handled things correctly, a lot of cooperation might be had. The idea of getting over on her appealed to him, and somehow as they talked, he started to think it just might be possible. They called on Barn Owl who readily agreed to a critical assignment, once he understood what Follows the Sun wanted to do, and why. That night Follows the Sun was back at the castle for another inspection.

"The following morning Mule, Cat, and Owl met again in the barn, Owl reporting his findings.

" 'I did just what you said,' said Owl. 'I had to go twice. Last night it was too dark to see anything so I had to go again very early this morning. The crystal is there all right. It sits in an open box that looks like it's lined with fabric. The box is on a small table. The only thing between the window and the box is about a thousand snakes. The window is about six feet above the floor, and looks big enough for me to get through, not that I tried.'

" 'Were you spotted?' asked Follows the Sun.

" 'I don't think so,' said Owl. 'Were you?'

" 'I don't think so either,' replied Follows the Sun, 'but I can't be sure.'

"Owl went up in the rafters to roost while Follows the Sun and Mule did more talking and planning. It took another three days to get everything arranged. They tried to not leave anything to chance, but realized that their information about the witch and her defenses was quite incomplete. It had occurred to Follows the Sun that the witch might be expecting an attack, since the man who was sent did reach the castle. In stopping him, she could have gotten information out of him, and in any case she certainly knew that she had the crystal. Presumably, she knew of its powers, and could even know of the coming blight. She may even have caused it for all he knew. He wished he knew what Man had done to try to get the crystal, and why he had failed. What he did know was all they could do is their best, and to put the rest in God's hands.

"Follows the Sun spent the day of the operation in fasting and prayer. The woman worried about him, and she noticed that many of the animals were restless. It was a warm sunny day, but later in the afternoon clouds rolled in from the west. After dark, lightning could be seen in the distance accompanied by rumbles of thunder, but it didn't rain. Eventually the woman went to bed. Well after midnight the animals assembled to receive their final instructions from Mule, and to hear an inspirational speech from Follows the Sun. They were all glad to have a chance to foil the witch, and if what Follows the Sun said was true, their very lives depended upon their success, so they thought they had nothing to lose.

"Quietly Mule led the way with Follows the Sun bringing up the rear of the procession, which also included several dogs, cats, ducks, geese, and a badger. Flying along with them were Owl, a golden eagle, and thousands of black hornets that had to lag behind because they made so much noise. Silently they broke onto the meadow, leaving Badger at the edge of the woods where he had prepared a tunnel. Waiting with Badger were several wolverines. While Mule waited at the moat, the other animals swam across. The dogs went around to the back of the castle where they waited by a door which was right where Follows the Sun told them it would be.

He had noticed that both times he had reconnoitered, men opened the door to take out trash early in the morning. The other animals went to the base of the tower where the crystal was kept. They tried to time things so they wouldn't have to wait too long, to minimize the risk of detection before they could spring their attack. And some animals are better at waiting quietly than others.

"At last the door opened. As two men began to carry out trash the dogs rushed past them into the castle. They had been told that there was no idea what the floor plan was or what exactly they would find. Their instructions were to all rush madly about, knocking over every candle and lamp they could find. One dog was to try to pull burning logs out of the fireplace. After creating as much confusion as possible they could try to get out, but not until they had succeeded in starting a fire. They also would have to fight the men and any monsters they might encounter. It was a dangerous mission, but the dogs were excited about it, and took pride in the importance of the diversion they would create.

"As it happened, there were only two men at first, and no monsters. The dogs rushed back and forth, knocking things over and biting the men who were fighting them off as best they could. And the dogs were fortunate again, in that one of the lamps they knocked over started a fire in some straw on the floor which in turn ignited curtains. As the kitchen filled with smoke more men arrived, and in the confusion the dogs ran out the door and away from the castle. They had been instructed to make certain they crossed the moat on the side of the castle opposite from the tower where the crystal was held. Mule had gone around to make sure they didn't get confused, and lead a pursuing party directly to the main action.

"As soon as he heard the barking Owl took off for the tower, leading the hornets to the window. Directly behind them was Eagle with Follows the Sun dangling from his talons. The hornets swarmed through the window into the room and attacked the snakes. The buzzing and hissing was fearsome as the floor boiled with writhing snakes who were confused and biting each other. Eagle deposited Follows the Sun on the window ledge, and before he could stop and think about what he was putting himself into, he jumped down to the floor. He couldn't exactly land on the floor as it was covered with squirming snakes, but land he did, and raced across the morass of slithering reptilian flesh to the table. Jumping upon it (it was also covered with snakes), he grasped the crystal in his mouth and ran back to the floor beneath the window. He was stung several times by hornets that had whipped themselves into a frenzy, but concentrated on grasping the crystal firmly in his mouth. He leaped to the window ledge, and without hesitation, he jumped. As he did so he heard a terrible shrieking noise and felt a blow to the side of his head. The crystal fell to the ground as he opened his mouth from the impact of what turned out to be the wing of a pterodactyl. Immediately, one of the geese gobbled up the crystal, and Follows the Sun picked up a stone they had brought with them in his mouth and made for the moat. Cats, ducks, and geese scattered every which way creating more confusion.

"Suddenly the moat was filled with crocodiles, but having no alternative, all the animals plunged in, and sad to say, they didn't all make it safely across. But Follows the Sun did, and once across, he raced to the edge of the woods, stopped to deposit his stone in Badger's hole, and then ran off. The pterodactyls pursued the animals, and right behind them was a horrible witch riding on a broomstick. As all the other animals scattered, the witch and her beasts surrounded the badger hole, which he guarded fiercely. A terrific struggle took place as the pterodactyls tried to dislodge Badger, only to be attacked by the wolverines. I'm sure you all know that Wolverine is about as dangerous a fighter as there is. A single wolverine can drive a pack of wolves off of a kill. You probably don't know about pterodactyls. They are huge flying reptiles. They look like enormous birds with rows of sharp teeth like the crocodile. It was a truly monstrous battle that raged for the rest of the night and into the morning. Once daylight returned, the witch returned to her castle. By noon, all the surviving animals had returned to their homes, that is, all except for Follows the Sun.

"The woman had slept very late for some reason, so when she ventured out things were pretty much back to normal. Mule seemed to be limping, and she was one duck short. She wondered if a fox had gotten it, but hadn't heard the dogs bark. Her Mister White Paws was nowhere to be seen, but that wasn't so unusual and she thought nothing of it. Word of the disturbance at the castle spread, but of course none of the villagers realized what had actually taken place. By afternoon, the witch's soldiers spread out asking everyone if they had seen a cat with white paws. Someone sent them to the woman. The soldiers demanded to know where the cat was, and she truthfully told them she hadn't seen him all day. The soldiers tore her place apart looking for the cat, with no luck. Another detachment had been sent to dig out Badger, and after doing so had reported to the witch that they had not found the crystal. The soldiers returned to the woman's home and tore it apart even more thoroughly, this time looking for the crystal, but found nothing. After dumping all her flour, cornmeal, sugar, and milk on the floor, digging up every inch of her yard and garden, completely tearing up her animal enclosures, throwing all of her clothing and linens on the ground, and breaking all her dishes, they left.

"The woman sat bewildered and in tears in what was left of her house. She couldn't understand what her poor little kitty could have done to enrage the witch so. She spent the night sitting by her fire, waiting for her Mister White Paws to return, but he did not. The following day neighbors came with provisions, dishes, and replacements for other things which had been destroyed, and helped her repair the damage and clean up the mess. The witch's soldiers returned with dogs, trying to pick up the scent of the cat, but were unable to locate him. That night the goose that had snapped up the crystal passed it out of her body. She was considerate enough to wash it, and then signaled to Owl, who flew to the top of a tall tree nearby and called out his strange cat-like call three times. Nearly a mile away the great horned owl heard him, and began hooting. The signal was relayed several more times until it reached the ears of Eagle many miles away. Eagle had carried Follows the Sun to his nest in the top of a tall tree the night of the raid. Our hero had to share the nest with two great eagles and their two ugly chicks. The eagles fed him fish, and carried him to a stream for fresh water. It was not a pleasant accommodation, but he was safe from the witch.

"Upon hearing the signal, Eagle once again picked up Follows the Sun in his talons and carried him back to the woman's cottage. Of all the difficulties he had faced on his journey, he realized that leaving the woman would be the greatest of all. It might have been safer to just pick up the crystal and go, but he could not leave without saying goodbye. He scratched at the door. Joyfully, the woman stirred from her bed and let him in. Follows the Sun rubbed against her legs, purring.

" 'Why you naughty boy,' she scolded. 'You had me worried to death. I was afraid that mean old witch had gotten her hands on you.'

"He walked back and forth in a figure eight around her legs, rubbing and purring. She lit a candle and poured milk for him. Eagerly he lapped it up. Then he washed his face, partly to get the milk off of his whiskers, and partly because he knew she loved to watch him do it. She sat in her chair gazing at him admiringly, and talking softly.

" 'So what did you do to get that mean old witch in such a stew? Did you eat her favorite mouse? I'll bet you did!'

"He jumped into her lap and nuzzled her while she softly sang to him her special Mister White Paws song. He had never known such love and affection. It would be hard to leave, but it troubled him more that she would miss him, than his missing of her. He at least would know where she was and why he had to leave. Maybe God could send him back in another incarnation, he thought. After some time of singing and stroking his fur, she dozed, as did he. Eventually, he could wait no longer. Jumping down, he pawed at the door until she let him out. It was another dark night, unusually warm and still. For some reason, she was drawn to step outside into her yard, carrying her candle, and watched Follows the Sun walk over to the barn. He said goodbye to Mule and Owl, and then found Goose. She led him to where she had hidden the crystal, under some straw in her enclosure. The crystal emitted a soft blue light, seeming to have an energy source of its own. He picked it up firmly in his jaws and trotted back to where the woman stood. He placed the crystal at her feet and meowed at her to pick it up.

" 'My, my, my,' she exclaimed. 'What a wonderful little stone!' She looked down at him as she began to comprehend. 'So this is what the soldiers were looking for! Where did you hide it? Did you steal it from the witch?'

"She continued to hold the crystal, now tightly in her fist, as she thought hard about what she was experiencing. Finally, she placed it back on the ground in front of Follows the Sun.

" 'Well, Mister White Paws,' she said, 'I always knew you were no ordinary kitty, but I didn't know what a special kitty you really are! I don't know what it is, but I can tell that you are involved in something of great importance.'

"He rubbed against her legs one last time, looked in her eyes, and meowed. He picked up the crystal again in his jaws, and walked to the center of the yard. Without any warning the sky developed an eerie glow, as lightning flashed furiously. A wind came up just as suddenly, nearly knocking her off balance. As she watched in amazement a whirlwind appeared between the house and the barn, and as it crossed the yard raising a vortex of dust, it enveloped her precious Mister White Paws, lifted him spinning into the air, and carried him off.

"The return of Follows the Sun to Paradise was a journey for which he had no memory. He remembered being in the woman's yard, and the very next thing he knew, he was back in his garden home. It was early morning. He hid the crystal in some grass while he sniffed around, trying to get his bearings. It was immediately apparent that something wasn't right. Even though there wasn't much light yet, what light there was had a strangeness to it. There was a kind of sour smell in the air, like decaying vegetable matter. As it grew lighter he could see that most of the plants looked sick. The edges of the leaves were curled, and they had black spots on them. The grass was brown, dry, and brittle. What flowers were in bloom were puny and drooping. The animals were listless. It was the blight! Maybe he was too late! In full daylight he could see a faint brownish-green haze in the air. There was no time to lose. Before long he had determined his location. He could reach the flat rock in a couple of hours.

"Without hesitation, he picked up the crystal and set off, but soon discovered that the going was not as easy as he had expected. As the garden had become diseased, thorny vines were taking over, thriving on the dank atmosphere. Not only was the journey difficult, but the air was so foul that he tired easily, often having to stop and rest. He had a feeling that today was the day of the summer solstice, and that it was imperative that he reach the rock by high noon. Bravely he struggled past the tangled brambles, as the sun climbed higher and higher in the sky. Finally the hill was in sight. The vines were especially thick here, but he managed to work his way through, until arriving at the hilltop, he was dismayed to find that the rock was covered by the dense vines. Hawk arrived just after he did, and together they struggled to clear the rock sufficiently to expose the groove where the crystal was to rest. The vines were tough, thorny, and difficult to clear, but by working furiously, when the sun was nearly at the apogee of its day's journey, they had made what they hoped would be a sufficient opening to let the light through. They could only pray that the whole surface of the rock didn't need to be uncovered. Follows the Sun went to pick up the crystal and was alarmed to find that in the short time he had left it on the ground while he cleared the stone, a tendril from a vine had wrapped itself tightly around it. Hawk managed to cut the tendril with his sharp beak, and together they unwrapped the crystal as quickly as they were able. Follows the Sun grasped the crystal in his mouth firmly, jumped on the rock, and placed it in the groove at the intersection of the two perpendicular lines.

93

It fit perfectly. He jumped off the rock and stood there expectantly with Hawk. They looked up at the sun that just then was disappearing behind a cloud. The wait was excruciating. Fortunately, he thought to look back at the rock and saw that the vine was growing so fast that it had already grown over the crystal. Jumping up, he grasped the vine in his teeth and pulled it off to one side just as the sun emerged from behind the cloud.

"Immediately a bright light bathed them as the crystal radiated life-giving energy, captured from the sun. The light was so intense that at first they were forced to close their eyes. When they opened them again, they could see the vines shriveling, their thorns dropping harmlessly to the ground. They felt waves of warmth, and the sickly haze lifted and vanished. As the crystal continued to burn brightly, the native plants took on their former healthy appearance. They stood upright, the leaves no longer curled or spotted. The flowers stood proudly on their stems, their colors once again vibrant. Songs of birds filled the air. Follows the Sun breathed deeply, feeling the fresh purity of the air nourishing his body and soul. He and Hawk looked at each other, basking in the glow of the crystal, victorious in their mission.

" 'You have done well, First Cat,' said Hawk.

" 'It was not I, but God, who made all this possible,' replied Cat. 'He acted through me, and through many others to save our world from the terrible evil. I feel blessed that he chose me to be a participant in this glorious drama.'

"He told Hawk of his adventures, including the two new names he had been given.

" 'Follows the Sun and Mister White Paws indeed!' exclaimed Hawk. 'They are both fine names. I have been admiring your new white paws. Which name do you prefer?'

" ' To be called Follows the Sun would be a great honor, should you be gracious enough to address me so. I reserve Mister White Paws for the woman whose love is greater than any I have ever known. It is true that obedience to God is its own reward, but I also know that God sent me to the woman, and her to me, so that we could love each other completely, in accordance with His divine plan, as a special blessing for our obedience to Him. And so it shall forever be between cats and people, that they shall dwell together in love, the human to serve the cat and provide for his needs.'

"Hawk was now perched on the rock, as the emanation of the crystal diminished gradually, and Follows the Sun jumped up next to him.

" 'Hawk, I thank you for your part in this struggle,' he said. 'I could not have succeeded without your help.'

" 'I did almost nothing,' answered Hawk. 'You are the hero in all this.' He paused for a few moments of reflection, looking up at the sun which was shining brightly as it made its way westward across the sky. Then he turned back to Follows the Sun. 'What will you do now?' he inquired.

" ' There is a small garden in Paradise, surrounded by a low stone wall,' replied Follows the Sun. 'Within the garden is a lovely cottage with a fireplace, a few simple pieces of furniture, and brightly colored curtains. I shall go there and lie on the low stone wall, warming myself in the sun, bathed by God's Grace, and wait for the woman to come home.'

"With that, Follows the Sun jumped off of the rock, sniffed at it one last time, and turned to the west. Hawk jumped into the air and hovered briefly over the cat.

" 'Goodbye, Follows the Sun,' he said. 'Maybe I will come and visit you sometime.' He rose higher in the air, flapping his strong wings as he flew first towards the west, and then returning in a broad arc to where our great ancestor stood, he swooped down, brushed gently him with his wing, and disappeared into the distance.

"At last he was alone, his task completed. Looking around one last time at the rock, the crystal, and the restored landscape, he breathed a sigh of satisfaction, and turning once again to the west he resumed his journey, that of following the sun."

There was a long silence after Talks with Wolves finished his tale. Slowly, one by one, we each rose, stretched, touched noses with him, and silently left the Gathering. It was almost dawn. Grits and I walked together through the neighborhood. Hardly any cars were moving yet, but here and there lights were coming on as people were getting up to get ready for work. We crossed a field, passed behind a row of houses, and soon were at Grits's back door.

"It has been a wonderful night," she said. "I didn't understand all of the story, though. Maybe we can talk later and you can explain it to me."

I said I would do my best, and left her. Truthfully, there was much in the story that I didn't understand myself, and every time I heard it I got new meaning from it. As I walked home in deep thought, I encountered a mother raccoon and her three cubs. I had been so absorbed that I allowed myself to get much closer than I normally would and overheard their conversation, or at least the very end of it.

"And so my darlings," she said, "that is why the raccoon is the favorite of all God's creatures, and this is why five times every day we thank God for the favor of being made in His Image."

They saw me, and she urged her cubs along, keeping herself between us. As I watched them amble off, it occurred to me that all creatures are born with the knowledge of God, but we can know Him only through our own experience. We all have our own mythology, but it is just that, mythology. We see as much as He reveals to us, limited by our own ability to perceive and understand. And what I understood then, better than I ever had before, was that whether we are cats or dogs, mice or men, black, brown, red, white, or any other color, striped, spotted, or solid-colored, large or small, alive or inert, intelligent or dull-witted, we are equally part of God's creation, and He dwells equally within us all.

I heard something rustle in the tall grass between our house and the house next door. I crouched motionless, my ears erect and pupils widely dilated. Soon, a poor unsuspecting little mouse appeared, and before it could save itself I pounced. Holding it firmly down with one paw, I quickly killed it. It was warm and lovely as I gently picked it up in my mouth and carried it to the back door for Archie. I then went around to the front of the house where I waited patiently on the lounge for him to open the front door and let me in.

12

It was poor little Jesus, yes, yes,
They whipped him up a mountain, yes, yes;
And they hung him with a robber, yes, yes,
Wasn't that a pity and a shame
Oh Lord,
Wasn't that a pity and a shame!

The Bat Mitzvah came and went in a rush of activity that I missed out on almost entirely. The events took place at Lenny's church, where I was never invited, and at their house. As I have explained before, I went over there often with Archie, but during the festivities whenever I tried to jump in the car with him he chased me away. So I can't tell you much about it except that it was a big deal. I heard that Lenny's relatives from out of town came, mostly from Mississippi and Alabama. Mama and Cora both managed to get to Lenny's church for the Bat Mitzvah. Mama's only reluctance had been her fear that someone would break into the house and steal her stuff while she was gone, so Mrs. Williams from next door and I house sat. Cora's only reluctance was her fear that possibly God would get her for entering a non-Baptist house of worship, but she wasn't about to let anyone else take charge of her mama. From what I could gather, Emily's job was to lead a prayer service in the Hebrew language. In the process of preparing for this she had to learn to read Hebrew, quite a challenge, I imagine. She also had to learn a lot about the Jewish religion. I can see the value of this in giving her a sense of her own identity, and where she came from. People (and cats) that grow up without knowledge of their own history seem to go through life lost. They seek happiness through power (territory), money (no feline equivalent), or sex or other thrills. They

97

struggle to feel important, sometimes succeeding briefly, only to fall back into self-doubt and depression. True happiness in this life is based on love of God, love of others, and thereby, love of self. The path to this destination is one of study, service, prayer, and meditation. Religion teaches people (and cats) about God through their own particular mythology, gives them spiritual principles to live by, and gives them rituals and ceremonies which help them feel connected to God and to each other in a strong and special way. Where people get confused with all this is when they believe their religion is the only true one, and feel entitled to force it on others, or see the beliefs of others as a threat. Some religions are atheistic ideologies, which is okay, I suppose, depending upon where they lead. People who are humanistic in their beliefs are as good and loving as the good Jews and Christians I have known. On the other hand, monstrous atrocities have been perpetrated in the name of other ideals (look no further than the Nazis and Aryanism.) Not that religions are exempt from the advancement of evil. The Spanish Inquisition is a good example of this, although I once heard Lexie say she read a book from the Marietta public library that held to the basic premise that the Spanish Inquisition wasn't really such a bad thing. The Christian church for most of its history has actively promoted the persecution and torture of cats, but I suppose somewhere someone will defend that as well. This heinous crime has its origins in the belief in the devil, which has its origins in people trying to understand the other side of good. All philosophies struggle with this question, and it is a principal theme of the story of Follows the Sun. The mythology of the Christian religion includes the belief in a powerful evil being, whose goal it is to gain control of the world by turning people away from God and His Son, Jesus. Both church and public officials, using fear as a means of manipulation to gain power, identified certain women (often suffering from mental disease) as witches, agents of the devil. And cats, particularly black ones (shudder), were said to be the evil minions of the witches. For no better reason than this, millions of cats have been tortured and murdered over the centuries. It has been only the last two hundred years or so that we have emerged from the dark ages, and cats have resumed their rightful place as the cherished and adored companions of Western civilization. Not that we are not still subjected to cruelty, but it is not systematic, nor is it any longer part of a confused religious belief. The mythology has become benign, confined to the secular Halloween phenomenon, and to a lingering superstition which no one takes seriously about black cats bringing bad luck.

As it developed, Emily's Bat Mitzvah marked a definite upturn in the family's life. Lexie had more energy, her color returned to normal, and her spirits were bright. The big smile was back. Lenny seemed like his old self again, except he seemed more content, and spent a lot more time with us. Archie was the healthiest and happiest I had ever seen him. He went out to AA almost every night, and he prayed and meditated regularly, although I must say he didn't have much of an idea of how to meditate effectively. At least he made the effort. He had a lot of energy, and although he went out a lot, he was also much more helpful around the house; and sometimes he even visited with Cora and Mama. With Cora, the subject of his recovery never came up, but he and Mama talked about it. They now had a spiritual connection they never had before. Cora still thought he ought to go to church, although she never did, but Mama seemed to understand that he was getting his spiritual needs met through AA, and he did read the Bible once in a while.

Emily was happier too. Part of this must have been because her Bat Mitzvah, and all the anxiety and study attendant thereto, was done with. I'm sure though, that it was mostly because her parents were doing well again. She was more fun when she and Lexie came over. Whereas before, she would go to the back and watch TV and isolate herself, now she was friendlier. Best of all, she took a renewed interest in me. She developed a passion for brushing my coat. It got annoying at times, but I liked the attention. She had grown quite tall by then, about the same height as Lexie. Everyone raved about how beautiful she was. And if Lexie had the Smile of the Universe, Emily was not far behind. It was a joy to be with her. She used to bring me little kitty treats to eat. Some of them were delicious, but others I had to force down and try to appear grateful. After one of the more disgusting morsels I began retching uncontrollably, the same way that I do when Archie gives me medicine. I was a little embarrassed, but the good thing about it was that she never tried that particular treat on me again. Sometimes she would bring a book to read or homework to do. I liked to crawl into her lap for a nice nap and plenty of stroking of my sleek black fur. She was in a new school this year and complained about all the homework, and many other things about it. It was called a high school, and I imagined it was on top of a hill until one day I was riding with Archie and he pointed it out to me. It wasn't higher than anything else in the neighborhood. I was a little surprised. Emily also enjoyed brushing Mama's hair. Mama usually wore it up, but it was actually long and beautiful. After Emily brushed it she would braid it in different ways. Mama still had her vanity, and enjoyed this immensely. It seemed to please Cora too. She didn't quite have the patience to fuss over Mama's hair like that. And also, when Mama was in better spirits, Cora's life was a little easier to bear.

It was starting to get cold again. The flowers were mostly gone, and the wind blew the falling leaves here and there. The blackbirds gathered in large flocks, and all the creatures busily prepared for winter. I was ten years old. Mama was ninety-eight. Talks with Wolves never would say how old he was ("many moons" isn't much information), but I knew he was older than I was. I carried on my activities much as usual, as peace and contentment returned to my life. The only source of discontent was Cora who could still find something wrong in anything. She seemed to live with guilt and regret about her life, although she never said so. She was more and more aware that her decision to move in with Mama and care for her after her retirement had been a costly one. She had been a school principal for many years, and worked hard, but she could always go home, take care of a few chores and dinner, and relax. She had gone from this to a retirement in which she worked constantly, didn't have her own life, and in which her own health had deteriorated so badly that even if Mama died soon, which didn't appear likely, she wouldn't be able to travel or do much of anything she had hoped to do with that part of her life. She wasn't even so sure any more that she would outlive Mama. So I guess she had her reasons to be bitter, and she dealt with it as best she could.

My meditations were more and more precious to me. It was a period of spiritual strengthening and renewal. I was at peace with myself and with the world around me. My years of prayer, meditation, learning from my elders, and general experience in life had brought me to a place of serenity. I had no illusions about living "happily ever after." We don't come to stay in this world, and as long as we are here, trials will come our way. I could truthfully say that I no longer feared the trials. I no longer confused the events and circumstances of my life with my life. My life was the spiritual path, and the events and circumstances were situations encountered on the path. I wondered sometimes if this was one of the things that set cats apart from people. I have never met a person who learned this distinction, and became free of fear. I do believe that people could also achieve this state of serenity, if they applied themselves with sufficient dedication to prayer and meditation, and found the right spiritual teachers.

Music continued to play an important role in my life. As always, I spent time every day with Mama listening to gospel songs. I also enjoyed Lexie's piano playing. She seemed to enjoy it more herself, and almost every time she came over to visit, which was several days per week, she played for a while. It used to be that she would have to be nagged into it by Mama, and usually refused. I never understood why. She must have been self-conscious, or she may have been letting some other fear or angry feeling get in her way. But now she never needed an invitation. She played classical music, show tunes, and religious music. She also sang beautifully. Mama usually stayed in her room and listened because it was so much trouble for her to move around, and her hearing was still good so there was no problem in her enjoying the music from the next room. My meditations began to include musical elements. I felt privileged, because most cats lack the capacity to appreciate music, and we certainly all lack the talent to produce it.

Winter arrived and lingered for a while. Lulu came down for Christmas, as did her brother, Arthur. There was much of a to do about everything, fussing at times, getting along better at others. Cora was her usual irate self when her sister was around, and as usual, Mama loved the attention. They exchanged presents and ate and talked a lot. I stayed away more than normal, and so did Archie. It seemed that he stayed longer at the fried chicken place, found more errands to run, and was at AA at least once per day. He had found some daytime meetings to go to, so he had a ready excuse to not be at home. He had never cared for Cora's brother or sister, and they had never gone out of their way to conceal that they didn't think much of him either. But they could be civil and tolerate each other for short periods of time.

Every once in a while Mama's pastor, Reverend Watkins, would come over for a visit. He never failed to come during the Christmas season. He was a large man, both tall and overweight. He was very dark-skinned, and dressed unlike anyone I had ever seen (except on TV). His shoes were particularly noteworthy, always being at least two colors, highly polished, and sometimes with cat toys attached. He always wore a fine suit, and much gold jewelry. He would come and sit with Mama in her room, visiting quietly for a while. I would sneak in and start playing with the tassels on his shoes until Mama would scold me and Cora would run me off. After a few minutes it was time for a prayer. Cora never wanted to come in for the prayer but she always did because she was afraid not to. When Archie was still drinking he would stay in his room (and no one invited him to join them), but now he would walk in and bow his head with the rest of them.

Reverend Watkins would start the prayer by asking everyone to bow their heads, extracting a large white handkerchief from his pocket as he did so. Then he would ask God to bless the house and everyone in it.

"Lord," he would say, "You know what a hard life it is for us here on this earth. You know our trials and our tribulations better than we know them ourselves. You know how we suffer from sickness and pain, sometimes not knowing how we can possibly get through the day. Sometimes, when we lie down at night, and thank You for getting us through, we wonder how we can get through one more day. Lord, we live in a world where there is starvation, cruelty, war in the streets, children growing up fatherless, orphaned by drugs and whiskey, mothers lost in the crack houses, a world which the devil calls his playground."

The folks assembled participated actively by frequently nodding their heads and saying "Amen", "Yes, Lawd", or every once in a while, "Thank you, Jesus." Reverend Watkins kept his handkerchief busy, mopping his forehead and switching it from one hand to the other.

"Lord, only You understand Your ways. You who have created heaven and earth, who put the sun and the moon and the stars in the sky, You know what is in our hearts and our minds before we do ourselves. Lord, we would be lost in this world without You, and Your Son, Jesus. We know that when we rise up in the morning, if we call upon Your Name, then everything will be all right. We ask that You be our Rock and our Shield and that You always be with us. All through the day when we get scared or lonely, when we don't know which way to turn, all we have to do is call upon the Name of Jesus, and You are there by our side. And when we lay down our head at night we give You praise and thank You for being there with us, all the day through. Lord there's no problem too difficult for You to solve. Yes Lord, You are our Protector and our Helper, our Bridge over Troubled Waters."

More amens, forehead mopping, and yes Lawds.

"Lord Jesus Christ, we ask that You bless this house and all who are in it. Grant them good health, prosperity, and peace, and instill within them the milk of human kindness to love and help each other, and all Your children on this earth. Teach them all Your ways, that they may know and love You. Prepare them to humbly follow You on the path of justice, mercy, and righteousness, until one day, in a time known only to You, they may join you in that Promised Land, and dwell in Your House forever. This we ask in Jesus' Name, Amen."

Sometimes the prayer would be much longer, but it was always delivered with great feeling. Other pastors would come by the house also from time to time to visit Mama and pray with her. I think they enjoyed it at least as much as she did. Mama was revered in the community for her longevity, her service to her church and community, and in the past, for her pecan pie. I strongly suspect that Reverend Watkins timed his visits so that he could count on getting something especially wonderful to eat. Mama hadn't baked for years, but Cora was famous for her lemon pound cake and her sweet potato pie. Even she was slowing down, but at Christmas time many people sent pies and cakes to them, and Lexie always baked a coconut cake for Mama, so the pastor was betting on a sure thing. Mama had " sugar", and usually Cora wouldn't let her have sweets, but with Lulu around, she couldn't be stopped. Lulu had a variety of comments to justify Mama eating things she wasn't supposed to, such as "Christmas only comes once a year" and "This little bit can't hurt her."

Every year at Christmas Archie would get a little artificial tree out of the storage shed in back and put it up in the dining room where Mama could see it from her room. He put some colored lights on it, and hung various cat toys from the branches. Truthfully, they weren't that great to play with, and I didn't mind being shooed away too much.

Lexie's tree was much more of a production. Every year she, Lenny, and Emily would get in their car and go out and cut their own tree, and bring it home. They would set it up in the family room, and decorate it with cat toys they kept in boxes in the basement. I used to enjoy going over there, sneaking in, and batting the cat toys hanging from the tree. Lexie didn't like it, but Emily was my friend who let me have my way. They always had a special Christmas present for me, usually a cat toy that smelled wonderfully of catnip. Emily was always giving me little things to eat, most of which were nothing for a cat to be interested in. They also lit candles at their house, and sang some Hebrew songs. Emily had a marvelous cat toy she called a dreidle. It was a little top with Hebrew letters written on each side. She would spin it, and I would chase it, knock it down, and bat it around. Then we would do it again, over and over. It was great fun.

Mama didn't get sick and have to be carried out on a cart this time after Lulu's visit, which was a good thing, but it didn't stop Cora from having a lot to say about her anyway, which we all ignored until she got onto something else. But Mama's birthday was toward the end of winter, and early on the morning of her ninety-ninth birthday I could hear the gurgling in her chest start in. She sat up in bed because she could breathe more easily that way, but pretty soon Cora called the men to come and get her. She was home a few days later telling everyone that she really had almost met Jesus that time. Each time she had one of her episodes, it took her longer to regain what health and strength she had. Lexie came over even more often to help, and a lady came during the day for a few weeks to help Cora out with Mama's meals, bathing, and so on. Archie did most of the cleaning and laundry.

By the time Mama got home spring was in the air. Migrating birds were coming through in large numbers on their way north. I particularly enjoyed the song of the white-throated sparrow, slow, lovely, and in a minor key. I had mentioned this once to some cats who thought I was crazy, lacking any sense of music themselves. Grits said that while she didn't really get it, she appreciated that I got it; and because she was my friend, she found my enjoyment of music to be one of the things she liked the most about me, even if she didn't understand just what there was to enjoy about it. Some of the migrating birds would stay and began to set up housekeeping, as did the permanent residents. So the songs of the mockingbirds, cardinals, wrens, chickadees, song sparrows, robins, and many others made springtime a special time for me, adding to the positive energy of renewal that I always felt at that time of year. I'm sure I was born in the springtime, so I was getting on to be eleven years old, not that cats really make much of a big deal about their birthdays the way people do. I was very much aware that I was progressing on my path, proceeding along the spiritual journey of my life. I was becoming something of an elder in my neighborhood. Talks with Wolves and Mrs. Baker had moved away, leaving Sampson as the oldest and wisest cat around. While the non-renegade cats in our area clearly now looked to him as their primary spiritual resource of a feline nature, I had now assumed the position, through no particular action of my own, as

104

number two. I actually was quite comfortable providing spiritual guidance to others, leading primarily by example, but also more than willing to share my experience of the Sun-path with any cat who was interested.

Some nights we would get together and Sampson or I would tell stories that we had heard from those who came before us. In my meditations I began, after all those years, to connect with my mother. I wondered whether she had passed into the spirit world, but felt that she had not. I also had visions of old wise, wonderful male cats, and felt a longing to know my father that I had not felt previously. It is part of the nature of the cat, part of God's plan, that we not know our fathers. It is an earthly void as well as a spiritual one. We are nurtured by the female, earth and mother, but the male we have to seek all of our lives. We sense it in the sky as the powerful sun travels across it each day. I have learned that the lack of knowledge of an earthly father is one source of energy which impels us to seek our spiritual path.

13

Precious Lord, take my hand
Lead me on, help me stand.
I am tired, I am weak, I am worn.
Through the storm, through the night
Lead me on to the light.
Take my hand, precious Lord,
Lead me home.

Spring led easily into summer. Life was in harmony, in a positive cycle, and I was content. But nothing lasts forever, and I thank God that I was far enough along on my path to be able to maintain my own sense of equanimity when the next round of trouble started.

By now, Lexie was back to her old self, and I had kind of forgotten that she had her health problems. But there was no reason for me to worry more trouble could come her way, more than to anyone else anyway. She was in the forty-fifth year of her earthly life. An incident when she was an infant exemplified the family conflicts she grew up with. Somehow, Jack and Constance Dobbins had been expecting her to be a boy, and were going to name her Charles Alexander. When their plan was disrupted by her femaleness, they couldn't agree on a name. Constance wanted to name her Inez Eugenia, after Mama, and Jack wanted to name her Carla Alexandra. Constance, being who she was, got her way on the birth certificate, but Jack, being who he was, called the baby Lexie, and it stuck. She had been a perfect child, always cheerful and polite. She loved going to church, except for the sermons during which Reverend Price would bellow and sweat as he warned about hellfire and brimstone being the wages of sin. She was a top student, and had graduated from the segregated high school on Lemon Street as valedictorian. She played the piano beautifully, and everyone said she was just about the prettiest girl anyone had ever seen. (I once heard someone comment that she was the most beautiful black woman he had ever seen, and I must admit I was offended by the remark, mostly because it was a black man who said it.)   Her childhood wasn't that happy, though, because her parents couldn't get along. Constance was overbearing, and had something to say about just about everything. Jack used to slip around and mate with other ladies. They didn't argue much, because when Constance would go into one of her tirades, Jack would clam up, go to the back of the house, and turn on his radio. Money was their favorite topic for disagreement. Because Constance brought home more money than Jack (she taught school, and he worked at the chicken processing plant) she thought it gave her the right to make all the decisions about spending. Naturally, Jack resented this. He hoarded his own funds so that he could do what he wanted to with his money. Otherwise, he thought it would go for some foolish purchase to furnish the house or for fancy clothes for Constance. Besides, he wasn't about to be emasculated by a woman just because she had an opportunity to go to college and get a professional job. He had grown up in poverty, the kind where you always wear second hand clothes, have to share a bed with two or three other children, and don't eat on time. Some meals had to be skipped altogether. He never knew who his father was either. His grandfather was a male influence for him, but unfortunately, he came along with a belt that fell on Jack and the other children with frightening force and regularity. It was all Pops knew about handling so many children, and nothing different from the way he had been raised. One of the greatest evils I have encountered in my life is the belief people have that their children need whipping. I wonder if it is left over from the experience of slavery.

Lexie's method of dealing with the trouble at home was to be as good as she could be. This left only the alternative route for her little brother, Jake, who was running the streets by the time he was fourteen. Constance had grandiose plans for her children, and wanted Lexie to go to Vanderbilt, where she did go for about a year and a half, until her money ran out. Jake never finished high school, got into dealing drugs and running numbers, got three or four females pregnant, and spent the better part of his twenties in jail. Constance was infuriated with Lexie for not coming back to Marietta when she ran out of money for school. Lexie had decided to stay in Nashville and work, which she did for several years. She had gotten a job with IBM and was doing very well, having received several promotions. She needed space from the suffocating rule of her mother, as well as the general dysfunction of the family. No doubt, she would have stayed in Nashville, except that on a visit home she met Lenny Solomon standing in a long check-out line at Kroger's, one thing led to another, and they got married. She was able to get a transfer to the Atlanta IBM office, but once she got pregnant with Emily she quit the job, it having served its purpose.

By the time she was back in Georgia she had fully developed her own life and personality, and so she was ready to set limits for Constance, who was prepared to resume the job of telling her how to live. Constance had nurtured a long-standing resentment of her siblings for moving away to Ohio, leaving her to take care of Mama and Papa all by herself. Not that they need much caring for initially, but as they got older there was more responsibility. They also had a tendency to interfere in her life more than their other children, because she was so convenient to them. Constance had expected that if it was her job to take care of her parents, then it was her children's job to take care of her when she got older. She certainly couldn't rely on her husband. As things developed it was obvious she was going to be taking care of Jake, instead of the other way around, and Lexie had the nerve to move to Nashville. Constance was ready to resume control of Lexie's life when she moved back, and there were some ugly words exchanged. She tried the guilt trip, the domineering matron trip, and other manipulations she considered appropriate to the situation. Her idea about family life was very much based on the quid pro quo notion that you do for your children when they are growing up, and then they do for you when they are grown. Lexie had other ideas including living her own life according to her own conscience. Jack Dobbins died of a stroke before she and Lenny even got married, and Constance died of heart failure about two years before I came along. Constance's explanation of the cause of her weak heart was that she had done so much for others that it had worn out. Lexie suspected it had more to do with her obesity and cigarette smoking, as well as her staying angry all the time.

So Lexie had liberated herself, had a brief but successful career in the business world, and established her own family. She went to the same church that she had gone to as a child, where she had many friends, and was involved in various projects of outreach to the community. She also went to Lenny's church sometimes. Emily went to both churches too, and had made her own choice to go to Hebrew school at Lenny's church and prepare for Bat Mitzvah. Lexie had a tendency to try to run Emily's life the way Constance had run hers, but Emily fought back as she neared her teenage years. Lenny didn't help matters at these times by referring to Lexie as Constance number two, and Emily as Constance number three.

None of what Lexie had experienced in her life had prepared her for dealing with cancer, other than her strong belief in God. Even this wasn't as helpful as it could have been because of all the preaching about hell she had been subjected to. Essentially, she was stuck in the way of thinking that if she was good, God would reward her. She was baffled by having developed a life-threatening illness at her age, and of course, she was frightened. Her biggest worry was dying before she had an opportunity to teach Emily everything she thought she needed to learn in order to cope successfully in life. She felt great sadness when she thought that she might not get to see Emily grow up.

When the cancer was found and the breast removed, the surgeon also removed some tissue under her arm, and there was one node within that tissue that also contained cancer. This was why she had to take the strong medicine that made her so sick. She was told that some cancer may have already migrated elsewhere in her body, and that the medicine was to kill it. There was a lot of uncertainty in all this. They didn't really know if it had spread, didn't know if the medicine would work if it had, and never would be able to tell unless she had a recurrence. She did understand that the longer she went without a recurrence the safer she would be, but even that would only be true if she lived five years without a recurrence. Once she recovered and was back to feeling like her old self, she tried to go on as though nothing was different. She found this to be impossible. Every time she had a little ache or pain she worried that the cancer was back. She tried harder to make Emily the way she thought she needed to be as quickly as possible. While Lenny was as loving as ever, she never completely adjusted to having part of her femininity taken away. Worst of all, she didn't know how to talk about it, and except for occasionally saying something to a girl friend, kept her musings to herself.

That summer Lexie was helping the church in a fund raising project. People had donated clothes for resale. Much of what was donated was pretty well worn and more appropriate to just give away (or throw away.) Lexie was helping to sort through the dozens of boxes, setting aside and

109

pricing the nicer things, and repacking the rest for distribution to needy families. She had spent several hours on her feet, and by the end of the day was aware of an ache in her right hip. For the next several weeks the ache would come and go. She mentioned it to Lenny finally, who insisted she see her doctor, which she resisted doing for several more weeks. By the end of the summer the pain was more constant, and when she finally went to see her doctor he ordered several tests, and then sent her to another doctor who ordered several more tests. I was not aware of any of this at the time, so I was as surprised as anyone when all of a sudden Lexie was back in the hospital. Once again great pains were taken to keep Mama from knowing what the real trouble was. Lenny had come over and told Cora and Archie quietly one afternoon while Mama was napping. I wasn't in the kitchen when he told them, so at the time was not in on the secret, but what I did know was that it was something bad. Cora came out into the living room crying. Gripping a handkerchief and wiping her eyes and forehead, she sobbed uncontrollably. Archie came in and sat with her, patting her massive back as she shook and trembled in her grief. When she was finally able to speak her words were, "Lawd, this gonna kill Mama."

The operation turned out to be much more of a production than the first one. She was in the hospital several days. Lenny came over and told Mama that Lexie had to have a hip replacement because of arthritis. Mama expressed mild surprise in that she had been unaware that Lexie had arthritis, let alone arthritis severe enough to require surgery, but she didn't ask too many questions, and seemed to accept the story at face value. Archie didn't let me come with him to visit her after she got home, and of course, nobody lets a cat visit someone in the hospital. So the first time I saw her I was astonished to see her ambulating with a walker, just like Cora and Mama did. She seemed to be in good spirits, had the same electrifying smile, and I still had no idea how sick she really was. Cora and Mama were overjoyed to see her, as they hadn't gone to see her either. Mama was just about unable to go out (except by ambulance), and Cora had nearly stopped going out herself. Her excuse was that she had to see about Mama, but the reasons had to do with her own arthritis, her anxiety about leaving Mama with someone else, and her embarrassment about her weight. In truth, she always made herself presentable and looked prettier than most women half her size, but she would never have believed it. Mama used to encourage her to go out, telling her that Mrs. Williams or some church member would sit with her. Mama would have loved to get a little breathing room from Cora once in a while. But I guess people just are the way they are.

After several weeks Lexie seemed to walk pretty well without the walker, and I more or less forgot about her having been sick again. Life went on as usual. Archie and I went to the fried chicken place every morning, I made my rounds of the neighborhood, Grits had another litter of kittens, winter was winter, and I still went out with Archie to Lexie's house or to an AA meeting once in a while. Emily was rarely at home any more when I went there, and she seemed to be busy on Sundays too, so she didn't visit us much either. But one thing I did notice about Lexie was that she didn't have much energy. One day I heard Cora and Archie talking about her going for more chemotherapy. They spoke in hushed voices and looked worried. One day when I was at her house I was startled to see that she could take her hair off. She had a wig like Mama did, except that it was dark in color, like her own natural hair. Later I heard folks talk about it. They said it was because of the medicine she had to take for the cancer.

That winter there was some other excitement at our place. Mama was to turn one hundred years old at the end of winter, and plans were being made for a big party. Cora was on the phone constantly about it, and she kept thinking of errands for Archie to run to see about this or that. It was some time after Christmas that all this got cranked up. Mama kept saying they shouldn't fuss over her; she was just an old lady who had lived too long. She couldn't have been more insincere, positively adoring the attention. Lexie and Lenny came over most Sundays for dinner. Lexie didn't look that great, but I didn't think that much about it, and Mama didn't even notice. For one thing, her eyesight was failing her. I used to hear her tell friends while talking on the phone that she was so sad because she couldn't read her Bible any more. Every once in a while one of her friends would come over and read some of her favorite passages to her. She knew many of them by heart, and enjoyed sharing the Holy Book, as she called it, with another human being. Mama was a highly social person. She did need some quiet time, but had a high level of need for contact with people. She had managed to remain active socially even though all of her same-aged peers were deceased, and she had become an invalid. She still had dozens of friends and acquaintances from church and elsewhere that she stayed in touch with.

I missed out on the party itself completely, as it was held in Mama's

111

church. For two weeks or so ahead of time there was constant activity at our place. The telephone didn't stop ringing until well into the middle of the night, every night. Archie unplugged his phone so he could get some sleep. I mentioned before that Cora and Mama stayed up late so it was nothing for them to get calls after midnight from the other night owls in the neighborhood. Invitations were printed, addressed, and mailed after endless discussions about who was to be or not be invited. Flowers were ordered, food was prepared, dresses were taken out of closets and tried on. Lexie was over often helping out. A lady from the newspaper came over and interviewed Mama who mostly wanted to talk about her church involvement. I did hear some things about her childhood that I had never heard before. You never would have known how hard Mama's life had been from her sanitized version of it.

The day of her one hundredth birthday was a Sunday, and the party was held in the middle of the afternoon. This was a good thing because it took Mama and Cora that long to get dressed, made up, and get their hair done. Well, for Mama it was wig done, and Cora never did use make-up. The traffic in and out of the house got on my nerves. I normally take a long nap late in the morning, but was constantly interrupted, so I went out and stayed away most of the day. It must have been quite a production getting Mama and Cora out of the house and into the cars, and then back again, but I missed the whole thing. It wasn't too cold that day, and there were plenty of sunny spots to stretch out. I did spend some time that day thinking about the span of one's life on this earth. We all have our path to walk, and never know how long it will be. I didn't think about my own longevity per se, but did reflect back upon my various experiences, and I must admit that I felt quite satisfied with what my life had been up to that point. I was grateful that God had made me a cat, that He had brought me to Archie's house, and that He had showed me so much of the spiritual way. For all its hardships, life had been truly wonderful.

When I got home that evening everyone was back. Mama and Cora were in their dressing gowns again, and Archie was in his room watching a little TV. There were flowers everywhere, and the phone just kept ringing. Later on Archie and I went out to an AA meeting, and I nosed around outside the church, leaving my mark here and there. I was still in a reflective mood, but mostly I think I was tired from the disruption of my routine. Later that night I hung out with Sampson for a while talking about longevity and how people make so much more of an issue of it than cats. He thought it had to do with the relatively weak spiritual connection that humans make with the Source of all life. They never get over their fear of death, as opposed to cats who understand death as just another aspect of life. As a natural part of God's design, it has to be good. People do have some understanding that the earthly life we experience is only one stage of a spiritual progression, but their ideas are rather distorted. They rarely get past the hope for things to come, into knowledge of things to come. So fear of death remains a powerful element in their lives. They also get so attached to loved ones that death seems a terribly lonely place to them, and this adds to the fear.

It was, I think, three days later that the grimness that life can be invaded our household. When Archie and I got home from our morning run Cora told him that Lenny had called, and that Lexie was in the hospital again. I didn't quite get what the problem was at first, but she had some kind of infection. The chemotherapy had weakened her resistance, and now they were giving her some other medicine. Lenny had thought she would be home in a couple of days. Well, a couple of days later he said it might be a couple more days. I had an intuition that she was seriously ill, supported I suppose by what I took to be the studied cheerfulness of my humans. Towards the end of the week I had a meditation which took me to a lovely garden on the bank of a broad river. The river was so broad, in fact, that I couldn't see to the other side, so that it could have been an ocean for all I could tell; except that I knew it was a river. There were several people sitting around, mostly not speaking to each other, and among them was Lexie. Somehow I knew that they were all waiting for a ferry boat to carry them across the river. Lexie appeared to be troubled. She couldn't sit still, and kept walking back along a path to a gate which crossed the lane at the back perimeter of the garden.. The gate was closed, and Lexie would stand there looking up the road. She tried the gate several times but it was locked. Finally, it opened, and she walked down the road away from the garden, quickly, as though she was gliding on air.

The following day another phone call left Cora deeply troubled, and she told Mama for the first time that Lexie was in the hospital with pneumonia. Cora told Archie, out of Mama's hearing of course, that Lenny had called to say that the previous night they had to put Lexie on a ventilator because her lungs had filled up so badly that she couldn't breathe on her own. I heard Lenny say much later that she had almost died that night, and the reason he knew that was the nurse had gone way out of her way to tell him that lots of times when people get that sick, they still recover. And when she came back on duty the next night he could tell she was surprised that Lexie was still alive. Every day Lenny called and spoke to Cora giving her an update. After several more days there was no effort made at pretense for Mama's sake. Mama cried a lot, prayed out loud asking God to save her grandchild, and sighed huge sighs. No one had much of an appetite. Of course, my outdoor life went on as per usual, doing all the catly things that I always do. But there was a dreadful tension in the house. This went on for weeks. Every few days the calls would cheer the folks up a bit, as she seemed to improve. Then the gloom would settle back in as she got worse again. Archie went to the hospital to see her fairly often, but Cora and Mama stayed at home, helplessly waiting and praying.

I had another meditation in which I saw a woman sitting on the front porch of a lovely little cottage. She was a small woman with gray hair. She wore a print dress covered by a starched white apron, comfortable shoes, and no jewelry. A gray tabby cat with white paws rested on her lap. Adjacent to her house ran a low stone wall beside which grew a row of hollyhocks, all in bloom. On the other side of the wall some men were building another house, and were nearly finished. The woman took a broom, and walked over to the new house where she began cleaning. The cat came along and sniffed around, marking various spots with his chin and his sides. I recognized the woman from the story I heard from Talks with Wolves, and the cat as Follows the Sun. After doing a little cleaning, the woman went back to her own house, got out a saucer of milk, and carried it out to her barn where there was a female tabby cat with a litter of adorable kittens who looked to be about six weeks old. She set the milk down for the tabby, petted her, and talked to her and the kittens.

After what must have been close to a month, Lenny called to say that Lexie had to have an operation. I didn't get it exactly, but I knew that in general operations involve doctors removing parts from people or cats. I couldn't figure out what part they were going to remove, but there seemed to be some hope that it would do Lexie some good. Later in the day he called back and I guess everything had gone well, based upon Cora's reaction. That night though, I had another meditation. I saw Follows the Sun and

114

the little woman standing in the lane in front of their house. Lexie came by, dressed casually in a flannel blouse, jeans, and sneakers. She looked vigorous and healthy. The woman greeted her and showed her the new house. Then she took her back to the barn where Lexie saw the kittens. She fell in love with an adorable little calico female, picked it up, and nuzzled it. After a while she put it down, told the woman she wasn't ready to stay, and she was gone.

Two days later Archie came home and told Cora that Lexie wasn't going to make it. He had left Lenny and Emily at the hospital. Rabbi Shapiro was still there. Cora didn't completely give up hope though, and she told Mama to keep on praying. That night I saw Lexie in a beautiful carriage being carried down a country lane by four strong white horses. Several carriages were in the procession, which stopped in front of her new house. A carpet of white flower petals had been laid from the lane down the path to her front door. The people who accompanied her lined up on either side of the carpet of flowers and greeted her joyfully as she glided along. Constance and Jack Dobbins were there, as were her brother Jake and Papa Porter. There were a host of other ancestors she had never met before; and there was Angela Knight, a child who had been good friends with Lexie when they were children. Angela had been killed by a car while riding her bicycle when she was eight years old. A profound sense of serenity prevailed upon the scene. The little woman was there with Follows The Sun and the calico kitten. There was plenty of fried chicken, greens, potato salad, and iced tea. Someone had brought homemade peach ice cream and pound cake. God was praised and hymns were sung. It was a vision that comforted me over and over as we all struggled though the next few months of our lives.

Lexie died on a Thursday morning, surrounded, as I later heard, by about a dozen souls praying and wishing her farewell. Reverend Lawrence, the associate pastor of her church was there, as was Rabbi Shapiro. Lenny and Emily were at her side bidding her a sweet journey, and Archie was there too. I was home when he arrived to give the news to Mama and Cora. He managed to say, "The Lawd has taken her home," but he couldn't get out another word. They all cried bitterly. Mama banged her fists on the TV tray. Cora tried to quiet her as she cried out, "My baby is gone, my baby is gone. Lawd have mercy, my baby is gone." The agony was so intense that I couldn't stand it and scratched at the door to be let out, but was ignored. After a while the phone rang, things quieted down a little and Archie gave me my freedom.

The next few days were rough around the house. The only break in the wailing came with planning for the funeral. This appeared to be as big a production as the hundredth birthday party had been, except that they didn't have as much time to get ready. It seemed as though there were two funerals. One took place at night at the funeral home, and the other one during the day the following Monday at the church. Mama insisted on going to the funeral home despite much fussing from Cora who couldn't stand to see Mama cry. She said she was afraid they would have to have a funeral for Mama too. Since Mama wanted to go to the funeral home, Cora went too, along with everyone else. I wasn't invited, and didn't really want to go. People have rituals for marking the event of the death of a loved one that cats don't need. I felt that I had gone part way down the spiritual path with Lexie, and that since death is only the other side of life, I felt as connected to her spirit as ever.

The day of the actual funeral was gray and windy. People were in and out of the house all morning. Mama didn't go. She had needed to see Lexie's body, I think to be sure that she was really dead, and so she could have one last look at her. She had no need to do it again. Naturally, Cora stayed with her as she was certain nobody could take care of her mama the way she could. Cora didn't deal with death very well anyway. She had heard too many sermons about hell, and had altogether too much guilt about her own past to be confident that God would have mercy on her when the day that comes to everyone would come to her. That afternoon flowers arrived in profusion along with dozens of visitors including just about every minister in town. Pies, cakes, fried chicken, jello molds, and hams likewise made their appearance. Mama insisted that Archie take most of the flowers to the hospital to cheer up the sick folks, and much of the food went to the shelter. It was a long day. I saw people laughing, crying, praying, praising God, and mostly being close and connected to each other as they tried to understand and accept the will of God as they endured this terrible loss in their lives.

14

Through many dangers, toils and snares
I have already come.
'Tis grace has brought me safe thus far,
and grace will lead me home.

Life was never quite the same after that, although outwardly Archie and
I went on with our lives much as before. He seemed to get even more
involved with AA and had started working with newcomers the way Jim had
worked with him. This was his method of distracting himself, I suppose.
Neither one of us could tolerate being at the house for too long. Mama
couldn't stop crying and wailing. Cora couldn't stand seeing her like that,
so she fussed at her and stayed upset herself. Cora's method of dealing with
her grief was to be even more involved in her caretaking of Mama, which
made Mama irritable. Nevertheless, this fussing did distract them some.

Lenny and Emily came over on Sundays. Emily usually brought a book,
and went into the back of the house to either read or watch TV. She had
gotten to a stage of her life where she had been fighting a good bit with
Lexie which I think is just part of what teenaged humans have to do as
they develop. People are much more complicated than cats. Even though
she had been in conflict with Lexie, she felt as though she needed her in
some ways more than she ever had. A number of women had tried to make
themselves available to her: neighbors, friends of Lexie, mothers of her own
friends, women from Lexie's church, women from Lenny's church, and
teachers. (Emily had entered the high school the previous fall.) Some of
these women were actually quite helpful to her, but only as a poor substitute
for her real mother. Emily and Lenny had always been close, and I'm certain
that Lenny was helpful to her during this early stage of her grieving. My

guess, though, is that she felt sad for him and didn't want to burden him too much with her own troubles.

My observation about kids is that the only people they really trust with their feelings is other kids their own age. Their fundamental premise is that adults are idiots who are right no more often than by random chance. Kids suffer from insecurity which has a lot to do with the biological changes they go through. They struggle to understand and be in control of who they are and what they feel. For Emily, an added complication was being racially mixed. While it was never a problem for her per se, it seemed to be a problem for others. While the popular crowd of white girls were superficially friendly to her, she wasn't invited to be included in their clique. One of them even told her that she couldn't let her come to her house because her father wouldn't allow it. By and large, the black girls didn't like her because she talked like a white girl, and because she was so pretty and fair skinned that the black boys lusted for her preferentially. Emily wasn't allowed to date, nor was she ready emotionally for a romantic or sexual involvement, so all the black boys thought she was stuck up. The white boys were interested in the white girls. Emily did make a few good friends at school, but never did find a natural peer group there. Where she found herself the most comfortable was with other Jewish kids. She was involved with the youth group at Lenny's church, but the problem here was that the church was in a different part of town. There were very few Jewish kids in her area of Marietta. So she spent hours daily on the telephone, without which, I have heard Lenny say, she would have gone insane.

Lenny walked around like a zombie for weeks. I guess he did all his crying by himself. I heard him talking about crying every day, but I never saw it. He said he cried in the shower, and he cried in the car. When he would come over on Sundays he would sit with Mama where they would listen to the radio. She always sat in her overstuffed chair at the foot of the bed, and I stretched out on the bed next to her. Mama would drum her fingers on the little TV tray set up in front of her chair. She called it her piano. After a few minutes of quiet conversation, Mama would go into her sermon. She talked about how God loves us, and that He knows what is best for us. We can't know what He knows, so we have to put our faith and trust in Him. We are the children and He is the Father. If we pray to God He will comfort us and provide us with what we need. These little monologues would go on for ten or fifteen minutes, and were always a cue for Cora to get up and leave, but it was obvious that Lenny enjoyed them. Mama and Lenny had become very close. She was the wise old grandmother that he lacked, and he was the devoted grandson that she lacked. They also thought a lot alike about spiritual matters. She once confided in him that even though she believed what the Bible said about Jesus, when she prayed she mostly prayed directly to God the Father of us all. Lenny had replied that he didn't think that any religion had all the answers, and that he was certain that if people pray to God with sincerity, that the prayers are always heard and answered. They both agreed that it didn't matter so much what people believe as it does what kind of life they live. They both agreed that Lexie was in a better place and that they would all be reunited one day. The truth of the matter was that for all her one hundred years in the church, Mama thought a lot more like a Jew than a Baptist. I don't even think she believed in Hell, although I never heard her say so. She believed that when people die they are called to account for their sins before God, and that there must be some consequences if the good deeds don't completely outweigh the bad, but she couldn't have believed that God would condemn people to everlasting suffering. There was too much love in Him for that.

Emily would join them for Sunday dinner. She did not enjoy these visits much, but Lenny was insistent. He told her that it was bad enough for Mama to lose Lexie, she didn't need to lose them too. I think it did give Emily a feeling of continuity in her life, and in a sense, a way of holding on to her mother. The dinners themselves were always good, but not up to Cora's previous standards. She just wasn't able to get around the kitchen fast enough to do what she used to do. Sometimes Archie would even bring home fried chicken, potato salad, and biscuits from the fried chicken place. Emily was good about giving me some of her chicken, and I never missed their Sunday visits.

It wasn't long before summer was upon us. The days were consistently hot and evenings not bringing the relief available in the spring or autumn. Sampson and I had decided to lead a Summer Gathering. Maybe it wasn't so much that we decided as we felt called to do it. The rhythms of life seemed to demand the experience, and we were now the senior cats in the neighborhood. Word must have spread quickly because even though no more than three or four days had passed between the time the calling came

119

and we actually did it, we had the largest turn-out I had ever seen for such an event. Sampson and I meditated and fasted that day, but didn't see each other until we were called by the chuck-will's widow after the stars were out. I tried all day to not think about what story I would tell, believing that God would move me when the time came. I was afraid that if I did too much planning, I would take control, and it would be Black Jack instead of God running the show. The metaphor I like for this is that of the Uncarved Block. I attempt to exist in the simplest state possible, and allow myself to be shaped by the Holy Spirit who has created me to do His work. They often play a spiritual on Mama's radio, the only line of which, sung over and over, is "I am who He says I am." Through years of meditation and other spiritual experiences, we are led to a deeper understanding of just who we are and what God's will is for us.

We gathered under a huge oak tree in the cemetery a few blocks from Mama's house. It was quiet here and we were less likely to be disturbed by people than over where we used to meet when Talks with Wolves led the conclave. The owls hooted softly overhead, and the locusts and their cousins played some good background music. High above the nighthawks soared and darted, making their little chirpy noises as they devoured mosquitoes and other flying insects. Sampson had brought a mockingbird feather, and I brought mint leaves I ran across earlier that evening. After we purified the feather and ourselves with the mint, Sampson gave me a sign and I began.

"A long, long time ago," I said, "there was a cat who lived in a far away place. He lived in a village with men who enjoyed his company, not only because of their instinctive love of cats, but because he would kill the rats that ate their stores of grain. He was a handsome black cat, larger than average, and with sleek, shiny fur. Now this particular cat was haughty. He was especially proud of his personal aroma, so much so that he called himself Honeysuckle. We all know that all cats use their personal odor to mark with, and we all like ourselves well enough, as is only proper, but Honeysuckle took self-love to an extreme. He began to think that he was the best smelling of all God's creatures, and that because of this he was set apart from, and above, all the others. He spent more and more of his time rubbing against trees, shrubs, and man-made structures in the village, and then sniffing the scent he left. He would grow intoxicated with his own essence, rolling around in grass where he had left his scent, and dozing off into a self-absorbed dream world. Gradually he let his duties slide. He was less and less interested in killing rats as this activity took time away from his personal ecstasy. The villagers became angry with him, and threatened that they would get another cat. He lost weight. He stopped grooming himself regularly, not wanting to remove the heavenly scent from his fur. He wanted every bit of it to mark his environment. Honeysuckle stopped meditating and praying, as he became the center of his own universe.

"Various creatures warned Honeysuckle that he was on the wrong path and headed for serious trouble. But as he ignored them and became even more self-absorbed, they let him go his own way. The dogs in the village found him harder and harder to tolerate, and they became aggressive towards him, forcing him to live outside the village limits. New cats came in and started killing the rats, taking over the void he had left. Eventually, Honeysuckle was close to death. His skin hung on his bones, his fur filthy and flea-infested. His eyes were dull, ears no longer able to stand up straight. He dragged his tail limply along behind himself as he crept through the forests and fields, grimly rubbing himself against everything he could. He became so malnourished that his senses were dulled, and he could no longer smell his wonderful aroma.

"One day he came to a clear pond, and as he walked to the edge to drink, he saw his reflection on the surface of the water. He was horrified at his appearance, and was flooded with the awareness of what he had become. He realized had he brought this terrible condition on himself. Honeysuckle repented in that moment. He knew that he was dying, and prayed to the Creator to spare him and forgive him for his arrogance. Because he repented, God took pity on him. A gray wolf appeared by Honeysuckle at the water's edge.

" 'Do not be afraid,' said Wolf. 'God has heard your prayer. He has sent me to tell you that even though you have been the most stiff-necked and arrogant of all His creatures, still He will forgive you. However, you will not go unpunished. Henceforth you will be the most evil-smelling of all those who walk the earth. You will be marked by a large white stripe down your back. Everyone will shun you, and you will have to eat the bark of the trees, and the insects and grubs of the earth. Your name shall be called Skunk, and your station in life will always be a lowly one, so that you and all God's children will know the terrible price of prideful arrogance.' "

My audience liked the story. Tails switched back and forth in appreciation, and two or three of the cats rubbed their chins on the ground and rolled around. They took some good-natured ribbing about being careful to not wind up with a white stripe down their backs. The air was still and humid, a hot June night. A siren wailed in the distance, accompanied as usual by the howling of a few dogs. Sampson stood up and stretched, taking center stage as I moved off to the side, settled comfortably on my brisket, and prepared to hear a good story. Sampson rolled in the mint leaves luxuriously, stretched again, yawned, and assumed a sitting position as he looked around to satisfy himself that he had everyone's attention. Holding the mockingbird feather under his right paw, he began.

"Once upon a time, many, many moons ago, there was a large village where people lived together peacefully. Now humans are among the least spiritually intuitive of all the creatures that walk on the earth, and therefore, easily subject to error. The village was prosperous and successful. They had an abundance of food, healthy children, comfortable homes, and good games to play, but they were aware that something was lacking in their lives. A village council was called to discuss the matter. Various ones spoke out with this or that complaint or suggestion, and after much debate the elders announced that it had been determined that the villagers needed a god to make their lives complete. A subcommittee was formed to decide who or what should be their god, and at a subsequent town meeting not too long afterwards it was announced that the lion, as the most powerful beast of the forest, was to be their god. They built a large temple for the lions, formed a priesthood to be the intermediaries between the lions and the people, and then went to the forest to invite the lions to come and live in their village.

"A solemn procession entered the village, the priests wearing their fine robes walking in front, with a long succession of lions following. The procession entered the temple, and all the people gathered outside to pray. Soon the lions told the priests that they were hungry, and men were sent out to hunt. It developed that the lions were a hungry lot, and the people were kept so busy procuring food for the lions that they had to let their own affairs slip. The lions, as it turned out, didn't like to stay in the temple all the time. They told the priests that they needed exercise, and they began to roam about the village, not particularly minding what they knocked over or where they left their waste. Some of the worshipers got too close to the lions and were mauled. The priests told the people that the lions were tired of antelope and pigs, and wanted to eat human children. The people refused, but the lions began helping themselves, and parents who fought them off were captured by the priests or killed by the lions. The priests enlisted the dogs to keep the people in line, and after some time many of the villagers escaped in a well-planned late night venture. They ran as fast as they could, carrying only the most necessary of items with them, and after several weeks arrived at a site they thought suitable to build a new village. They had been pursued by the priests with their dogs, but only a few had been captured and dragged back.

"The settlers of the new village worked hard to reestablish a normal life, and after a year or two, comfort and prosperity returned. They had to admit, though, that something was lacking in their lives, and what was at first rumblings here and there in quiet corners, gradually became a clamorous roar as the people cried out for a god they could worship. At a village meeting a debate raged about what had gone wrong with the previous arrangement. One faction held that they never should have made the lion their god, because he was too dangerous. Another faction took the position that the problem had not been the lions, but rather, the priests. They never should have given a group of people the power to come between them and their gods. A third group agreed with both of the first two groups, arguing against both lions and priests. In the end, they could not agree, and split into two groups. One group left the village to set up their own, new village, where they could select a god of their own choosing. The remaining group decided to make the lion their god again, but this time not have priests. There was to be a class of people who waited upon the lions, but they would have no ritual responsibilities, and no dogs. As you might imagine, the lion worshipers fared as badly as they had the first time, and of those people that survived, some managed to join up with the other faction, and the remainder scattered to a nomadic existence.

"Now, in the village of those people who had left rather than accept the lion as their god again, there was discontent. Once again, the people were aware of the emptiness of their lives, as the longing for a god arose among them. As they had been joined by some that had escaped a second time from the lion-gods, there was general agreement on not worshiping lions again. One young man suggested what no one had thought of before. He was a clever fellow who had the gift of drawing pictures. He offered to make an image of a lion that they could worship. This had obvious advantages over real lions, and it was decided to let him make an image so that they could have a better idea of what he was talking about. The young man got busy with his task. Being limited in materials and tools, he did some experimenting, and finally found that he could form shapes out of mud. He mixed earth and water in different proportions, used different kinds of earth, tried adding dried grass and other materials to his mixture, and finally was pleased with his technique. He then produced a life-sized male lion figure, standing erect and haughty, and staring ahead as though surveying his subjects. The people were amazed. 'This clay lion shall be our god,' they all said.

"A large shelter was built for the statue so that it would be protected from the rain. The young man convinced them that the lion-god needed tending and suggested that he be appointed its caretaker. This was readily agreed to. As time went on, the young man created more lion statues, saying that their god needed the company of other lions, and also that this would give them several gods to worship. He got so busy tending to his duties that he told them that the gods had requested that he attend them full time. The people agreed and began to bring him food. Then he explained to them that the gods wanted gifts so they would have prosperity, and be protected from all danger. He built an altar for the purpose of sacrificing animals to the gods, who gradually became more and more demanding. After a time more attendants were required. The young man began to wear fine robes at the insistence of the gods, who likewise identified the most beautiful young virgins in the village to be a harem for him.

"The people were happy. They had gods that protected them from danger, provided them with good hunting and gathering, and kept diseases away. The gods didn't tear down their village, maul their citizens, or eat their children. It was true that these gods required more maintenance than they had expected, and that they had to develop a system of taxation to support the whole operation, but it seemed worthwhile. They developed rituals with the assistance of the young man, which pleased the gods and brought even greater prosperity. He told the people that the lion-gods were so pleased with everything that the young man was to be known henceforth as High Priest. As time went on many children were born to him, he acquired more wives, and conscripted a large number of aides, male and female, to carry out all the many duties of the priesthood.

"Grumbling began to be heard as the burden of supporting the religion grew, and those who spoke out against the lion-god or his High Priest were severely punished. As time went on, his sons began to assist him in his priestly duties, and they were likewise ordained as priests. A severe drought came, and for the first time there was a shortage of food. The High Priest told them that the gods were angry with the people for holding back on their offerings, and had demanded double taxation or the drought would remain. Rumor had it that the lion-gods might soon demand human sacrifice to quell their wrath.

"The people grew more frightened and miserable. It must be said that there were people in the village who never had thought too much of the clay lion-god, and who secretly whispered among themselves. They couldn't quite understand where the idol derived the power to affect the weather, provide good hunting, and keep diseases away. One of these people was a widow who lived at the edge of the village in a poor lodge with her little girl, who was around ten years of age. Now, Morning Breeze was a happy child, despite being poor and fatherless. She helped her mother with their goat and chickens, and worked in their little garden. She enjoyed playing games with the other children, and was popular with them. Morning Breeze had a sweet disposition, never complained about her chores, and everyone agreed that she was the prettiest of all the children..

"Suddenly, a crisis developed in the village. The gods had sent a new sign of their anger. The first grandson of the High Priest was born with the split upper lip of a rabbit. Moreover, there were six fingers on each hand (instead of five), and a large strawberry-looking thing grew on his back. The infant could not nurse properly, and died after a couple of weeks. The people of the village were very afraid, and the little girl was now old enough to be at least somewhat aware of the troubles.

"Now, the lodge of Morning Breeze and her mother was close to the edge of the forest. Morning Breeze used to enjoy wandering into the forest after all her chores were done (only the children of the priests went to school). She was an observant child, and knew much about the habits of the animals there. One afternoon after eating a little lunch she went off into the forest. She had a favorite place where she used to lie down on the soft pine needles next to a burbling little brook. Here she would gaze up at the forest canopy, looking for tiny patches of blue sky, and watch the dragonflies, ants, birds, rabbits, and other forest creatures busily pursuing their lives. On this particular day, as she lay there she dozed off, and some time later was awakened by the feeling of something rubbing against her. When she opened her eyes she beheld a creature which was something like a lion in its appearance. Its ears were pointed instead of round; it was no bigger than a young lion cub, was darker in color than the lions, and had subtle striping down its sides. In other words, it was a cat. No one in her village had ever seen a cat before. The cat rubbed against her with his sides and chin, purring loudly.

"Morning Breeze was delighted with the new animal which was so beautiful and friendly, but at the same time she was uneasy, thinking it might be the cub of a much larger animal which might be dangerous. She talked to it and stroked its fur, carefully surveying her surroundings as she did so. Eventually she told the cat that she had to go home, and as she walked off the cat followed her, all the way to her lodge. When Morning Breeze's mother saw the cat she too was worried that it might be the cub of a much larger animal, and she scolded Morning Breeze for bringing it home. The child explained how she had found the strange animal, and that it had followed her home. She begged her mother to let it stay. He mother had misgivings about it, but told her that the cat could stay until morning, thinking that it would probably wander off by itself in the night.

"When Morning Breeze lay down on her straw pallet that night, she pulled the blanket up under her chin, and the cat climbed right up on her chest and went to sleep. In the night, she had a dream in which the cat spoke to her, and it was so realistic that she never was certain whether it had been a dream or not. In this dream, Morning Breeze was lying awake in bed with the cat, which washed itself thoroughly, and then sat up, looking straight at her.

" 'Morning Breeze,' said the cat, 'my name is Nathaniel. I have been sent by the Great and Holy Spirit, the True God, to warn you of danger. Your village is under the spell of the evil lion-cult, and it is doomed. The High Priest is frightened and angry because of the deformed grandson he was given. His council will advise him to attempt to pacify the lion idol with human sacrifice. God has noticed the goodness of you and your mother, and sent me to save you. In three days the priests will come to your lodge to take you before the High Priest, who means to offer your life up to the lion-god. You and your mother must quickly prepare for a journey to a place I will show you. No one else must know. As a sign to you, I will leave a mouse just outside the entrance to your lodge where you will find it in the morning. As a further sign, the next morning there will be a snake outside your lodge, and on the third morning I will leave a rat by the entrance. On that morning

126

you and your mother will each gather your blankets and follow me into the forest. I will lead you to a safe place where you can live peacefully. And I will lead you to God.'

"The next morning, Morning Breeze awakened feeling troubled. After a moment she remembered her dream. She looked around the lodge where her mother was already busily preparing their breakfast. The cat was gone. Unable to resist her curiosity, she looked outside and there, just outside the entrance to the lodge, was a dead mouse. She wanted to tell her mother of her dream, but was afraid that she would be scolded for making up such a tale. So she held her tongue all that day, not even responding when her mother asked her why she was being so quiet. On and off during the day, the cat reappeared. Neither she nor her mother said anything to anyone about the cat for fear that they might get in trouble, and no one else in the village seemed to notice it either.

"That night Nathaniel curled up with Morning Breeze and went to sleep. He came to her again in a dream. His yellow eyes appeared especially stern to her, as he conveyed to her the seriousness of his message.

" 'Morning Breeze,' he urged, 'you must tell your mother of my warning. There is no time to lose. Tell her of the signs, and she will believe you.'

"Morning Breeze told her mother of her dreams right away when she awakened the next day. Together they went to look outside, and sure enough, there lay a snake just outside the door. But her mother did not believe her.

" 'Morning Breeze, why do you trouble me with such foolishness?' she exclaimed. 'Now go and milk the goat!'

" 'But mother,' pleaded Morning Breeze, 'do you not see the snake outside the door? And do you not remember the little mouse that was in the same place yesterday? What I have said to you is true! You must believe me!'

" ' There is nothing so strange about a dead mouse or a dead snake,' her mother answered. 'Do what I say and milk the goat right now, and not a word of this foolishness to anyone!'

"The truth of the matter was that the woman was deeply troubled about her circumstances. There was barely enough food, no rain in sight, and the people murmured about frightening things. She supposed that Morning Breeze had heard some of these rumors, and her imagination had gotten the best of her. And it was strange that the cat had appeared. She had never seen anything like it before. She wondered where Morning Breeze could have gotten such an idea as the True God. While she had never heard of such a thing before, it struck a harmonious chord within her. As the day went along, she couldn't stop thinking about these peculiar events and ideas. And so, as her heart was opened she felt the stirring of a spiritual connection to something loving and wonderful.

"That night she kissed Morning Breeze and covered her with the blanket. The cat appeared, curled up next to the child, and proceeded to groom himself. The woman went to bed, but she could not sleep. Maybe they were in danger from the priests. She felt quite helpless, and didn't know what to do. The idea of following a strange little animal into the forest with her daughter, and leaving everything behind, seemed ludicrous. She felt so anxious that she could feel her heart pounding inside her chest, and had trouble getting enough air to breathe. She remembered the expression that Morning Breeze had used, 'The Great and Holy Spirit, the True God.' With this thought in her mind she felt some relief from her anxiety. She had been alone for several years, caring for her daughter all by herself. There was no one to discuss this with. Now she felt powerless as their lives seemed to be slipping into great danger. She imagined the priests coming to her lodge and dragging off her precious daughter. The more she thought about it, the more real it became. Her heart pounded again as she felt crawling sensations in her skin. She fell into a restless sleep, in which she dreamed of an altar before the great lion-god. Morning Breeze lay upon the altar, her feet tied together, and hands tied behind her back. The face of the statue was impassive as the High Priest ascended the altar, his white robe shining in the sun. He carried a knife, the long blade of which flashed with the sun's reflection. The priest stood over the child holding the blade high, and as he plunged it towards her heart, she heard Morning Breeze's piercing cry of 'Mother, don't let him!'

"The woman was jolted awake in a cold sweat, the horrible image burned into her brain: the impassive idol, the evil priest, her helpless child. She thought again about the cat and the Great and Holy Spirit, the True God. In her desperation, she made a decision. If the rat was there in the morning, and the cat led them into the forest, they would follow. The next thing the woman knew, Morning Breeze was shaking her awake as light streamed through the small window in their lodge.

" 'Mother come look!' demanded the child as she practically dragged her mother off of her pallet and to the door. There, just outside the entrance

128

to the lodge, was a dead rat. 'Mother, it is Nathaniel's sign! We must follow him!'

"The woman looked around. The cat was not in sight. She gazed up at the cloudless sky as if looking for guidance.

" 'You go milk the goat, my child,' she sighed, 'while I prepare some breakfast for ourselves. Then we will decide what to do.'

"Morning Breeze was overjoyed. Her mother was actually thinking about the meaning of the signs. She wished that Nathaniel would return soon. When she returned to the lodge she saw that her mother had prepared an especially large breakfast of both eggs and porridge. As she glanced excitedly around their abode, wondering what would happen, Nathaniel entered, jumped onto the table, and licked up the little bit of egg that remained on her plate. Jumping down, he held his tail high in the air as he rubbed up against first Morning Breeze's legs, and then her mother's. He purred loudly doing so, and then lay down in the middle of the floor to groom and wash his face. He then walked to the door two or three times, and lay back down, staring at them upside down with his yellow eyes.

"The woman shut her own eyes tightly and took a deep breath. There was a long silence that followed, until she was ready to speak. A decision had been made. A mother must protect her child. She might be crazy, but if Nathaniel headed into the forest, she and Morning Breeze were going to follow him. She looked around her lodge. The instructions had been to take blankets, but nothing was said about food. She had no idea where they were going or how long it would take to get there. Gathering up a loaf of bread, she turned to her daughter.

" 'Fold up your blanket, child,' she said, 'we must be on our way.'

"Excitedly, Morning Breeze folded her blanket. As soon as this small task was accomplished, Nathaniel stood up, and they followed him out of the lodge and into the forest."

It was time for a break, as some of us had grown a little stiff and restless. Sampson told us to stretch, and a couple of the younger cats got kind of frisky and started wrestling with each other. It was late at night. The distant sounds of human activity had diminished. It was as dark as it ever gets in the city as the moon had set on that cloudless night. I got up to stretch, and wandered off a short distance by myself. I rubbed my flanks against a gravestone and sniffed around in the grass, deep in thought. Soon it was time to return for the rest of the story.

"Nathaniel led them quickly through the forest," continued Sampson. "After a couple of hours of plunging ahead they came to a broad stream, and Nathaniel began to lead them upstream along the bank. The woman stopped for a moment to consider their situation. She thought she had heard something. She strained her ears to hear what Nathaniel had been hearing for quite some time: the sound of dogs barking. How would they be able to elude the dogs?

" 'Step into the stream, my child,' she said as she picked up Nathaniel in her arms. 'The dogs won't be able to follow our scent if we wade through the water.' They continued upstream, the woman leading the way carrying Nathaniel, with the child following behind. Afraid to stop, they waded without resting until long after they could no longer hear the dogs. Morning Breeze and her mother both assumed that if they were going wrong Nathaniel would give them a signal. Instead, he quietly allowed himself to be carried as he alertly watched where the stream-path took them. They came to a place where a tree had fallen part way across the stream, and it was there that she decided to stop for a rest. She and Morning Breeze ate some bread, and found some berries growing along the bank that they also ate. Nathaniel took a quick nap, but soon was pacing back and forth on the log, nudging them both with his head, indicating that it was time to go.

"The sun was low in the sky when they broke through the forest into a broad meadow. They had been wading somewhat uphill for some time, and now found themselves among low hills and rocky outcroppings. Nathaniel jumped down, sniffed the ground for a moment, and then purposefully led them towards some hills to the north. Before dark, they found a cave where they spent the night. They traveled several more days, the humans surviving on roots and berries, and Nathaniel, of course, found plenty of good hunting.

"One day they saw smoke in the distance. Nathaniel led them in the direction of the smoke, but as they got closer the woman became very anxious. She and Morning Breeze kept their distance while Nathaniel walked into a clearing where they saw a strange hut. It was made from large poles arranged in a circle and lashed together at the top, covered by animal skins. They could smell meat cooking, and longed for a taste, as they had grown weary of the roots and berries. They watched as Nathaniel circled around behind the tipi, and a few minutes later he reappeared, followed by another cat, and returned to their hiding place.

" ' Oh, mother, just look!' exclaimed Morning Breeze. 'It's another creature just like Nathaniel!'

"The new cat was marked very similarly to Nathaniel, what we now call a tabby cat. This cat, however, was a female. She rubbed against Morning Breeze and her mother, and flopped over on her side, looking at them upside down. Morning Breeze petted her and rubbed her chin. As they did so, the woman looked back into the clearing as a boy emerged from the tipi. His skin was bronze, darker than theirs, and his hair was jet black. He wore a skin tunic that came to his knees, and his feet were bare. He tended the fire and the roasting meat. Soon thereafter, coming from the opposite side of the clearing, they could see a man approaching. He was tall, had similar coloring to the boy, and wore trousers made of skins. He wore nothing above the waist, and also was barefoot.

" 'Father, father!' cried out the boy excitedly, 'Nathaniel has returned.'

"The man greeted the boy quietly, and looked around the perimeter of the clearing. Even though they appeared to be well hidden from view, the man looked exactly in their direction, and spreading his arms wide in a welcoming gesture, he said, 'Do not be afraid. Come and join us. We have been expecting you.'

"The two cats left the woman and her daughter, and re-entered the clearing. Tentatively, Morning Breeze and her mother followed. The people approached each other, father and son, mother and daughter. They gazed at each other for a long time without speaking. Then the man gestured to his guests to sit by the fire, where he served them meat. They ate in silence, gazing at each other, wondering what the others were thinking.

" 'My name is Red Horse,' said the man. 'Little Eagle is my son. We have been living here by ourselves for five winters. Little Eagle was in his seventh winter when we were driven from our village by the elders who would not accept our ways. The Great Spirit had made Himself known to me through signs. I taught what I had learned to my wife, and she followed my lead. Our village worshiped fire and thunder. There were evil practices that displeased the Great Spirit. He showed me signs that taught me that He was the Great and Holy Spirit, the True God. We would not participate in the rites of our village, worshiping fire and thunder. Now fire and thunder are powerful, but they are not gods. The True God had made them, as well as all that is in the world. He made this known to me. We were seen as enemies of the village because we would not worship fire and thunder. The elders feared that their gods would bring harm to the village because of us, and they plotted to kill us. The night before we escaped we were visited by these cats. It was a sign, and in a dream I was ordered to follow these beloved creatures of the True God. And so we escaped, pursued but not caught. My wife died the following year. I placed her in a cave, rolled a stone in front of it, and the boy, the cats, and I have come to this place. My son has grown strong, and learned well all that I have taught him. Soon he will be a man.'

"He paused in his story and stirred the fire. Morning Breeze was filled with wonder. The man had spoken of the Great and Holy Spirit, the True God. His tale of escape was very similar to theirs. The cats were God's messengers.

" 'God has provided us with everything we have needed up to now,' continued Red Horse, 'but humans are meant to live together, male and female. I have prayed, and He has heard me.'

"He looked at the woman. 'What is your name?' he asked.

"The woman looked down. She had lived without a man for many years. She felt afraid, but at the same time felt stirrings within her. It seemed as though this Great Spirit was offering her a new life. She was eager to learn more, and this man could teach her.

" 'I am known as Lily,' she said, 'and my daughter is Morning Breeze.'

" 'You shall be my wife,' Red Horse replied, 'and I shall call you Little Bird Woman. We shall live together in harmony, in the company of the Great Spirit, and teach our children of His ways until He gathers us up from the earth to His Own Home.'

"So this is how God made Himself known to humans. Red Horse and Little Bird Woman lived together for many years, and were blessed with many fine children. As Little Eagle and Morning Breeze matured they also became man and wife, and raised many children, a new race of people who knew God. Nathaniel and his female, Eve, likewise mated and brought many kittens into the world. And it is because God ordained that it should be the cat who would be His agent to save Red Horse, Little Eagle, Morning Breeze, and Little Bird Woman, and use them to make Himself known to all men, that man is forever in debt to the cat and obligated to serve him."

It was still pitch dark outside. An early morning breeze was stirring, a hint of coolness in the air. Leaving the cemetery I noticed a bat silently flying overhead. My route home happened to take me past where Talks with Wolves used to live, and I lingered there briefly, trying to pick up some of his essence. The memories of him were strong, but I didn't feel him at all. The mantle had been passed on to Sampson, just as some day it would fall on someone else. We don't come to stay. We only pass through this world, have our brief moment to live and to love, and then travel on down that mysterious path, sweetly shrouded in hope, leading to new worlds of life and love.

15

So I'll cherish the old rugged cross
Till my trophies at last I lay down;
I will cling to the old rugged cross,
And exchange it some day for a crown.

Cora was wrong in the literal sense. Lexie's death didn't kill Mama. I don't know where she got the strength to survive her agony, but survive she did. Lexie died in April, and the rest of spring and all that summer were pure torture. Mama cried so much that she got infections in her eyes, and suffered with terrible headaches. Cora was beside herself. She couldn't bear to see Mama suffer. I think it fed into her sense of inadequacy and helplessness, but on the positive side, she stayed so upset with Mama's grief that it distracted her from her own. The intensity of the grieving seemed to abate somewhat by autumn, but this didn't last long as Lexie's birthday was in November, and this got Mama started all over again. Of course, the birthday was followed immediately by Christmas, and once that was past we were encroaching on Mama's birthday which was the event she associated with Lexie's final illness and death. Mama said she didn't want the Christmas tree that year but Archie put it up anyway, and I think she was glad to see it. Lulu came down from Ohio, and she and Cora had one of their more acrimonious encounters which was good because it gave Mama something else to be upset about.

Archie and I went once in a while to put flowers on the grave. Lenny used to bring stones as well as flowers. He and Emily continued to come over nearly every Sunday, and his parents even came occasionally. The radio played non-stop with church announcements, gospel tunes, preaching, praising of the Lord, and callers to the station with their Bible questions for the "Ask the Pastor" segment. They also had contests for the listeners who had to guess something right and also be the twelfth caller, thereby entitling them to some prize, such as tickets to a gospel music festival. I enjoyed the music as always, and found that it comforted Mama for me to be there with her while she listened. It gave her a sense of the connectedness of all things, that a cat could enjoy "God's music" with her, and a deeper awareness that God reaches much farther than even she had ever known. Lenny enjoyed the music with us from time to time, and even liked the preaching. I must admit, some of the preachers had style.

Archie and I would still go over to Lexie's house occasionally for Archie to fix something for Lenny. After the first few times, I just stayed outside; the house felt so empty, it made me sad. Things in some ways were just as Lexie had left them the night she went to the hospital. Most of her clothes were still in the closet, and some of her cosmetics remained on the counter. The first time we went over was a few weeks after she died, and while there I still felt her presence somewhat, but when we went back the next time I didn't pick up on anything of her essence. One nice thing did happen. Lenny brought home a kitten. She was black and white with eyes that eventually turned green. She was extremely vocal and nosy, and a bit of a scairdy-cat. She stayed out of my way when I came over, and they never let her outside. Lenny was afraid she would run away or get hit by a car, and he didn't want Emily to be upset about another loss. Emily called her Sylvia, and they seemed to enjoy each other's company. Emily spoiled her rotten, if you ask me.

After Christmas we had a little bit of real winter which gave everyone something to talk about. Then, before you knew it, things in nature were stirring once again. A lot of females come into heat in late winter which always gets my juices flowing. I got into some good fights with stray toms. Even at my age I could take good care of myself. Most of the more permanent resident males would act tough, but back down pretty quickly to me when it got right down to it. The truth is that the fighting is mostly for bragging rights because the females will mate with whomever they please, and they are not that impressed by shows of machismo.

Mama's one hundred-and-first birthday was a day of mixed feelings. Mama as always loved the attention of those who called, came by, and sent her flowers. Brother Parker and his crew wished a happy number 101 to Mother Inez Porter in Marietta and sang her the happy birthday song. Cora had called it in to the station, and Mama was very pleased, although she pretended not to be and scolded Cora for doing so. Mama cried on and off most of the day, more than she had been. Then we had the build-up to the anniversary of Lexie's death. Everyone said it was hard to believe that Lexie was already gone a whole year. When the day came, Lenny offered to take Mama to the cemetery. Cora's eyes popped but before she could say anything Mama had already said no. She told Lenny that she wasn't able to get around well enough, and that she would see Lexie soon enough, as she was old and would be going home soon.

But go home soon she didn't. Mama hadn't even had to go the hospital that entire year. Sometimes her lungs would start to fill up with fluid, but Cora would give her an extra pill right away, and that seemed to take care of it. Lenny and Emily continued to come over most Sundays. Archie and I continued to go to the fried chicken place every morning. He kept busy with his AA activities, and I still went with him once and a while. Sometimes men came over to the house and Archie would talk to them about drinking, not drinking, and about "the program." He and Lenny still hung out some and had good talks. What they referred to as the program appeared to be the collective spiritual principles and practices of AA. Neither one of them ever had a slip that I knew of, and I'm sure I would have known.

Another year went by. The second round of anniversaries and holidays was less intense than the first year, but painful nonetheless. Emily came over with Lenny one Sunday, mad as she could be. She didn't say a word during dinner and kept glowering at Lenny. After dinner he and Archie went out on the front porch to talk, and Mama asked Emily what was wrong. Apparently she actually already knew, and as I listened to her talk quietly to Emily I realized that Lenny had a girl friend, and Emily was hurt and angry about it. Mama was very sweet to her, and so was Cora. They explained that Lenny was lonely and needed someone in his life. They weren't actually telling her anything she didn't already know. I think it did help Emily some because they were so kind to her about it, and because they supported what he was doing. If they had been offended then this would have fed into her own indignation. Emily got most of her support from kids her own age, but she certainly needed this kind of loving adult attention at times, especially from women.

Mama gradually grew weaker and her eyesight grew worse. She hadn't been able to read even the large print Bible for years, and now TV was a complete waste of time. Her hearing remained keen, and she had no difficulty hearing the radio guys singing her a happy one hundred-and-second birthday. Everyone remarked at how mentally sharp she remained. She didn't miss anything, never repeated herself, and could still carry on an intelligent conversation. She listened to the news, and was completely up on what was going on in the world as well as locally. She often said that she had prayed to God that she never lose her mind, and clearly He had heard her. Even though all of her contemporaries had died she was still connected to a great many people who were delighted to make a big deal out of her birthday. There was cake and ice cream, and a steady stream of folks came and left all day long. Several of the area ministers came by to pray with her, and for the sweets that they knew would be offered. They never had to ask. A dish of ice cream miraculously would appear, accompanied by some kind of cake or pie, and sweet tea.

But after these events I began to notice she was sleeping more, and her appetite was falling off. Cora fussed at her to eat, and she tried to force herself. The second anniversary of Lexie's death was not nearly as intense as the first one. Mama and the others were moving towards acceptance of their loss. Archie and I put flowers on her grave again, and Lenny and Emily each brought a stone. Lenny and his girl friend seemed happy together, and Emily was more accepting of her. She was a very nice lady, and particularly fond of cats. I think Lenny met her at his church. One thing that Emily did like about her was that she didn't have any children of her own. This meant she wouldn't have to share her daddy with any other kids if they did get married.

Early one morning, with spring in full flower, Mama awakened with her lungs filling up. Cora gave her a pill, but it didn't seem to help, so without waiting too long she called for the ambulance. The men came, gave Mama oxygen, and carried her out on their little cart. I knew she wasn't coming back. It was her time, and I could feel it. They would probably keep her alive for a few days at the hospital, but God had called her, and she was going home. Not that she was ready. As much faith as she had in God's mercy, she was still afraid to let go. To a cat, it is clear that our time here is part of our journey, that God is our Constant Companion, and that when we leave the world as we know it we progress to another dimension of existence where God is even more immediately present and comprehensible. We leave our companions in this world with few regrets, and never think about unfinished business. For people it is not so simple. As I have said before, they are among the least spiritually intuitive of all the creatures. Their spiritual perspective is clouded, as though they are looking at life through opaque glass. So they remain anxious in their uncertainty about both what they are leaving and where they are going. And it was in such a state of doubt and fear that Mama left this world. Cora was with her at the last. Mama had hold of her hand, and her grip suddenly became remarkably strong as she said, "Cora, don't let me die." Cora later said that almost immediately thereafter Mama's grip relaxed, her facial expression changed into one of peacefulness, and she let out her last breath.

Mama's passing was an event that stirred up a lot of activity for a few days. Lulu came down from Ohio with her family, as did Arthur and his wife. There was plenty to argue about: what picture of Mama to put in the program, what music to have at the funeral, which vase to put which flowers in, and so on. Cora was outraged that Arthur had brought his golf clubs and played a couple of rounds, and she had a great deal to say about it. There were extensive discussions about who was going to get what of Mama's. None of this was any too pleasant, and I made myself scarce. I wanted to be alone with my thoughts anyway, and was able to find much peace under the hydrangeas and amongst the grasses of the fields. I was pleased to hear that they did sing "The Old Rugged Cross" at the funeral, since it was Mama's favorite, but I don't think much of anything else went the way she would have wanted.

Of course, not too much was the same after that. True, Archie and I went on as before. But other things were so different. The radio was turned off. I missed the constant acknowledgment and praising of God by Lee Williams, Hezekiah Walker, Mahalia Jackson, The Mighty Clouds of Joy, and so many others who sang and preached their hearts out. Cora was lost with nothing to do, and was too crippled to do anything anyway. While in one way she had given up the last good years of her life for her mother, at least she was able to feel good about what she had done. And knowing her, she would have found a way to not enjoy her life, whatever the circumstances. And Mama was gone. When someone is there all of your life, and then suddenly is gone, a void remains which is palpable. I missed her much more than I had expected. The sounds of her grunting as she moved around, the scraping and clanking of her walker, the sound of her voice, all were replaced with silence. The near-constant ringing of the phone quieted into a couple of calls per day for Archie. I would jump up on my favorite place on Mama's bed, and she wasn't there sitting in her chair next to me. Cora fussed at me a little more than usual, I suppose as a distraction to her grief as well as her strong predisposition to fuss at somebody or something. Her life was changed more completely than the rest of ours, and I think she came around to the notion that there was no more purpose to her life.

Late that summer I heard a familiar gurgling sound, but this time it was Cora's lungs filling up. Archie called the ambulance, and off she went on the cart. She was back home several days later with her own bottles of medicine. She claimed they took thirty pounds of fluid off of her. She was weak but feeling much better. Archie was normally good about leaving her alone to do what she wanted to, but they started to argue about what she ate, and how she took her medicine. She had always known better than the doctors what was good for Mama to eat, and which pills Mama should take, and when. Mama had been a co-conspirator in this rebellion. Archie had noticed that the pills Cora was supposed to take twice a day she only took about every other day. She said they made her dizzy. Another pill she didn't take at all because Mrs. Goodman said they were dangerous. The doctor had given them to her sister and she died. Cora took supplements she had bought from Mrs. Johnson who said they were good for her heart and her kidneys. Her diet consisted almost entirely of cereal, grits, cheese, and yogurt. After a while Archie gave up and just let it go.

Lenny and Emily still came over Sundays, but not as often. For one thing, Emily was now sixteen and more involved in her own life. She even had her own car. Once in a while Lenny's girl friend, Janie, would accompany them. As I said before, she was a lovely little woman who liked cats. Just before Christmas Cora's lungs filled up again. This time she was gone for a long time, and when she came back she was very weak. Archie wasn't able to do everything for her, and a nurse would come during the day. The nurse would bathe her, feed her, give her medicine, help her to the toilet, and keep her company. Archie had to help her at night. They struggled along like this for a short while. Then Cora said nothing tasted good, and she stopped eating. Archie, the nurse, and everyone fussed at her and told her she had to eat, but she took in very little, mostly juice and a little yogurt. She grew weaker, and one night she fell coming back to bed from the bathroom. Archie was helping her, but she just seemed to collapse.

He was unable to get her off the floor and into the bed, so he had to call the ambulance. The men came and decided she needed to go back to the hospital, so off she went on the cart. Luckily, she hadn't broken any bones. Archie got a special bed for her, and when she came back he had nurses for her all the time. It was clear where all this was going. When people (or cats) are ready to die, they often stop eating. Her disposition actually improved, and she was sweet to the people who cared for her. She started using a bedside commode instead of struggling all the way to the bathroom, and then that got too difficult, so she used a bedpan.

It was notable how few people called to ask about Cora or came by to visit her. She had grown up in Marietta, lived her adult life mostly in Ohio, but had been back in Marietta more than ten years. You would think she had childhood friends still around, but there were none. She had come in contact with scores of Mama's friends, but had managed to either antagonize them or just not connect with all but a very few. Whenever Archie's friends came over she had made herself scarce. She didn't belong to a church, had no community-based activities, and had made little effort to interact with their neighbors. She had no children, and had antagonized every one of her relatives. Lexie would have overlooked her faults and remained devoted to her, but she was gone. So it was mostly Archie, Lenny, Emily, one or two other occasional callers, and the hired nurses and aides who she was left with as her human contacts. The contrast between her and Mama in this regard was striking. I have heard a song in which the idea is expressed that people who need people are the luckiest people in the world. I think it would be more accurate to say that people who are able to make loving connections with other people are the luckiest people in the world, but that line would ruin a great tune.

Things in the neighborhood were changing. Mrs. Williams next door had lost a foot due to sugar, and she and Mr. Williams had gone to live with their daughter somewhere. The house was sold, and rented out to a family with small children who enjoyed playing with me. I hadn't had the pleasure for many years since Emily was little. Grits was getting very arthritic. I think getting hit by the car was catching up with her. Mrs. Johnson's eyesight was getting bad and she couldn't do her own marketing any more. Mrs. James who did it for her wouldn't buy the frozen anchovies for cat treats because they grossed her out, so that little piece of heaven was eliminated from my life. Other people and cats came and went. Archie and I still went to the fried chicken place every morning. The sound of the trains rumbling through town day and night was a constant. The birds, mice and squirrels still built nests and raised their young. The raccoons remained as arrogant as ever. Dogs barked. Men congregated on street corners after dark, smoking cigarettes, drinking wine, and calling out to the young women who walked by.

Cora lasted nearly until the second Christmas after Mama died. She and I both knew she was going home before Archie did. Her mind remained sharp until the end. I had heard her start to talk more to her nurses about her life, her Mama and her Papa, her work as an educator, her little accomplishments and disappointments. It was a rather sanitized and superficial encapsulation of her life, but one that made her comfortable as she prepared to move on. Her disposition mellowed still more, and she even enjoyed my visits to her sick bed. I would jump up on the bed with her and she would talk sweetly to me and stroke my fur. As I have said before, she was a complicated, conflicted, and often disagreeable woman, but I always liked her.

She passed quietly one night in her sleep. Lulu flew down, and she and Archie made all the arrangements. Lulu still had a lot of friends in Marietta, so it was mostly her friends and Archie's friends who called. I did not see one tear shed the entire week. Lenny came over, of course, and Emily made a brief appearance at the house so we played together for a little while. Arthur flew down the day of the funeral and then flew right back to Ohio the same day.

It was amazing how quiet it was at the house with just Archie and me living there. Just as I was getting used to it there were more complications. I had never thought about who owned the house we lived in. As far as I knew it was my house. But apparently, the house had been owned by Mama. She had changed her will to provide that Cora could live there as long as she wanted to, at Lexie's insistence. Now that Cora was gone, the house fell to Lulu and Arthur, who put it up for sale almost before Cora was cold. It wasn't long before it sold, and Archie and I had to find another place to live. During the three weeks or so that we had to vacate Archie had looked around for a little house to buy in the neighborhood. However, we soon had a more serious problem.

I had come home from a night of tomcatting and what-not late one night in early February. As I crossed the street in front of our house I saw a dead opossum in the street, his pale face glowing white in the moonlight. I caught a little mouse, deposited it by the back door, and then came around the front to lie on the chaise lounge and wait for Archie to let me in. But he didn't let me in. The sun was high in the sky, the day had hit its full stride of activity, and no Archie. I clawed at the door with no result. I was confused, hungry, and upset. Being a cat, I eventually lost interest in what I was doing, and began to wander around the neighborhood. I got so hungry that I was able to focus long enough to have squirrel for lunch, but then got to worrying again, so I went home to scratch at the door again around mid-afternoon. With no result again, I stretched out to wait, and after a while Jim came by. I later learned that he had become concerned when Archie had failed to show up for a noon AA meeting that he was supposed to chair. Jim had returned to work and called the house several times with no answer, so he left work as soon as he was able, and came over. He couldn't get Archie to answer the door either, went around back and saw that the car was in the driveway, and then went next door for help. The next thing I knew a police car arrived, and after much discussion and pounding on the door, they broke a window and one of the officers climbed in.

Soon the door was opened and I charged in. Archie was lying on the floor next to his bed. He was in terrible shape. The right side of his face was drooping, he had soiled himself, and he seemed unaware of what was going on even though his eyes were open. Quickly an ambulance arrived, and this time it was Archie who was carried off on the cart. Lenny arrived before they carried Archie off, looking about as upset as I had ever seen him. I wasn't any too calm myself. I rubbed up against Archie, but he was so unresponsive that I backed off. It was a weird experience. I heard Lenny and Jim discuss a few things, they made a few phone calls, and Jim found some plywood in the shed to temporarily fix the broken window. Lenny told Jim that he was going to take me home with him until they could see how Archie was doing. He carried my litter box, dishes, and a bag of cat food out to his car, and after cleaning up some he picked me up and carried me out to his car. And so for the first time in nearly sixteen years I was separated from Archie and taken from my home.

The change took some getting used to, but I am pretty adaptable, and got into an entirely new routine. Many things were different. I was rarely let out at first, as Lenny had the absurd idea that I might get lost or try to find my old house. It is true that some older cats don't tolerate relocation very well and do get lost, but I am not just any cat. Sylvia didn't take too kindly to what she regarded as my encroachment on her territory, and was decidedly unpleasant at times. I had never had to share a house with another cat before either, so I was not as gracious as I could have been. I had all the comforts I could ask for, and the opportunity to spend more time with Emily, even though she was gone most of the time. I started sleeping with her at night. I would grow restless in the early morning when it was time to hunt, and amused myself by prowling around the house. Once in a while I was lucky enough to find a roach or a centipede, but there was nothing that you could really call hunting.

After a time, on the days that Emily came home after school she would let me out for an hour or so, so I wasn't completely cut off from the out-of-doors. I was already acquainted with the neighborhood cats and dogs, and had my spots I liked to visit. There were times that I thought about Grits, Sampson, and the old neighborhood, but most of all I missed Archie. He was in the hospital for the longest time, and then was in a nursing home where I wasn't allowed to visit. I would hear Lenny talk on the phone about him occasionally, which was my source of information. He had started to talk some, and was getting exercises for his arm and leg. They were getting him out of bed so he could learn how to walk. He was in my thoughts and prayers constantly. I sent him a lot of positive energy.

Lenny always left the remote where I could get it, knowing of my peculiar habits, so this provided me with some amusement and contact with the outside world. Some evenings Emily would do homework assignments using the computer. Curious as always, I watched her, and one day when I got tired of napping and watching TV, I started to mess around with it. However, I still hadn't gotten the notion to tell my story, so all I was doing was pushing different keys to see what would happen. Lenny used the computer too. Sometimes he did work-related tasks, and he did a lot of venturing into cyberspace. Emily got on the internet fairly often as well. It didn't take me long to get the hang of it, and soon I was visiting various web sites and chat rooms. It is amazing what you can pick up browsing on the net.

Sometimes Janie would come over, and occasionally Lenny's parents. Emily had a boy friend who came over quite often, but overall, the level of traffic through the house was quite a bit less than at Mama's. I meditated as always, and never failed to say my prayers. I think it was mostly the adherence to these spiritual practices that helped me through this difficult transition in my life. I never felt sorry for myself nor questioned God's will. I was grateful for my life and the many comforts and blessings I did have, and the gratitude itself was a blessing.

Just about the time I was getting used to things they changed again. Emily graduated from high school that spring, and this was a big whoop-de-do. All of a sudden there were no end of phone calls, visitors, and excitement. Emily was home a lot for a few days, and then was gone. She had a job working at a summer camp, and as it turned out, never did return much. At the end of the summer she went away to school, coming home only occasionally. So it was just Lenny, Sylvia, and me, and since now I almost never got outside, I ran the risk of actually getting bored, something that had never happened to me in my life.

I don't know exactly how the idea came to me to write my story. But I had so much time on my hands, and I had the means and the skills. I think it came to me in meditation that God wanted me to do something with my unusual gifts, and from this notion gradually emerged the decision to write my story. It has been a lot of fun for me, and has given me greater understanding of things to put it into words. I am saving it on the computer, but I have been careful to not let Lenny know what I am up to. I'm afraid that if he catches on that I am using the computer he will unplug it when he is not using it for fear that I will mess it up. And there is no way I will be able to handle that plug.

I'm not sure what else to say now that I have brought my story up to the present. I guess I should mention that Emily came home for Christmas, and I get to see Archie now. He is living in a nice place where he has his own room, and his own things. He walks with a cane, and can't do much with his right arm. There is a dining room where all the folks who live there can take their meals. He talks fairly well, and is in good spirits. He gets lots of company, and Lenny and several others pick him up for AA meetings, or to go out to eat. I can visit him there but they don't allow cats to live there. Once a week Lenny and I pick him up and we go to the fried chicken place where we hang out and do our respective things.

The latest big deal is that Lenny and Janie are getting married. She has already started moving some of her stuff into the house. She has a couple of cats, so that should make things pretty interesting around here. I'll have to set them straight about a few things right away. Emily isn't coming home for the summer. She will stay at school and work. I think she is staying away mostly because she thinks she'll be uncomfortable with Janie here, but I can tell they are doing much better in their relationship, and have no doubt that they will come to see each other as a great blessing in their lives. I suppose as time goes on I'll have more to say, but for right now I think I deserve a good nap.

Epilogue

The editor asked me to write a brief explanation of how I found this story, and where it came from. The way I found it was that one day I was going through the files on my hard drive to see what I could get rid of to make more space available. I saw a file named "I never knew who my father was." It didn't sound familiar, so I brought it up. It is so hard to describe what it felt like to read the story, as it was partly the story of my own life. I assumed that Emily had written it. I ran across it about five years after Lexie died, when Emily was a college sophomore. When I showed it to her she was just as surprised as I was, and said there was no way she had written it. I guess we finally believed each other, so who did that leave? There were only a few people who come over to the house to have access to the computer. Archie still comes over when I bring him, but he only comes for visits, and would never have had the time to write the story. My parents come over for visits, and also have a key, but I don't see how they could possibly have known enough about the family to write it. Besides, they have their own computer, and would have done it at home. Neither one of them is much of a writer anyway. My next door neighbor has a key to the house, but neither she nor her husband could possibly know enough about the family to do this. Janie could have written it, but she says she didn't, and she wouldn't lie about it. The fact is, I don't know where it came from.

Maybe Black Jack really did write it. He was around for everything that happened.. It gives me a strange feeling to think he may have busted me that day I used cocaine for the last time. It gives me an even stranger feeling to think that he understood our human lives. You basically think of your pets as just being there, not as thinking that much about what goes on. Anyway, I could hardly ask him, partly because he obviously wouldn't say anything anyway, but mostly because by the time I ran across this, he had died. Maybe the reader would prefer to think he has gone on to the spirit world. It was not long after Janie and I got married. He kind of stopped eating, and we took him to the vet, who said it was cancer. Eventually he got pretty weak and sick. All he would do is lie around looking pitiful. When it started to look like he was in pain we all talked about it. I brought Archie over for one last visit, and then took him to the vet to have him put to sleep. He is buried in our back yard. We marked his grave with a couple of bricks, and all had a good cry that afternoon.

So I don't know where this story comes from. What I can tell you is that it is an authentic account of our family life. It was Janie who convinced me to have it published. She said it's a good story and it doesn't matter if people believe the cat wrote it or not. She and Emily broke the story down into chapters, and they also put in the lyrics from the gospel songs you saw at the beginning of each chapter. They thought it would add something. Otherwise, the story is just as I found it on my hard drive three years ago.

Emily is now in grad school studying horticulture. She wants to make things beautiful like her mother did. She is doing well with her life. Janie and I have been happily married for almost three years. After some rough times, she and Emily are getting along great with each other. Archie and I still are clean and sober. We go to a meeting together every week, and we have him over to the house pretty often. He is getting along great, really. He can't drive or button his shirt, and sometimes he fumbles around for a word, but otherwise he is the same old Archie. He is getting the biggest kick out of this story getting published, and I think he is the only one who totally believes that Black Jack wrote it. Oh, and one more thing. Not long after Black Jack died Archie called us up and said that Mrs. Johnson couldn't take care of Grits any more, and could we adopt her. So Grits is our cat now. She is very sweet, and a little overweight. We sort of keep our eye on her, but she never shows the slightest interest in the computer.

Lenny

Editor's note

I liked this manuscript immediately when I read it, and I was intrigued that it was by an author I had never heard of. When Lenny Solomon sent it to me, he hadn't written the epilogue, and I had no idea that he was going to insist that he had not written the story. After talking to him, however, I decided to meet with him. I visited Lenny and Janie in their home. Emily was home from college. I won't say that they have convinced me, but what I will say is that Lenny didn't write it. He is not a writer. Quite frankly, I am tired of trying to figure this out, and I have decided to let go of it. We think we have a story here which makes for enjoyable reading, and will let our readers decide for themselves what to think about its authorship.

About the Author

Michael Cowl Gordon was 60 years of age by the time he published this, his first novel. He acknowledges that for most of his life he has allowed his commitment to family and the demands of his addiction medicine practice to interfere with his writing career. It was five years after the death of his beloved wife, Gena, that he decided to write the story that has become *"Memoirs of a Southern Cat."* What started as a project to facilitate his healing has turned into a story with universal appeal, and if the world had to wait until his beard was white to hear what he has to say, it was well worth it.

·

Printed in the United States
29979LVS00002B/94-1008

9 781418 447274